Between a
Rock and a Hard
Place

God's Holding Pattern

DR. HERLDLEEN RUSSELL

CROSSBOOKS

CrossBooks™
A Division of LifeWay
1663 Liberty Drive
Bloomington, IN 47403
www.crossbooks.com
Phone: 1-866-879-0502

Scripture taken from the King James Version of the Bible.

First published by CrossBooks   04/30/2014

ISBN: 978-1-4627-3656-0 (sc)
ISBN: 978-1-4627-3655-3 (hc)
ISBN: 978-1-4627-3657-7 (e)

Printed in the United States of America.

This book is printed on acid-free paper.

Contents

What People Are Saying About "Between A Rock And A Hard Place"...

Dr. Russell has penned a powerful and biblically based synopsis of how to navigate through God's preparation process (*Between a rock and a hard place*) for your life. She brings clarity to the seasons of the journey and identifies roadblocks that hinder.

Dr. Barbara McCoo Lewis
Assistant General Supervisor- International Department of Women Church of God in Christ, Inc.

Jurisdictional Supervisor- Southern California One
President/CEO Southern California COGIC Economic Development Corp
President/Ceo Barbara McCoo Lewis Ministries

"Dr. Russell is affectionately known to many as 'Dr. Mom.'" After you read this book you will understand why. Her wisdom and counsel is excellent. Reading this book is like sitting down with 'mom' and talking about a personal problem, as only 'mom' can do, she provides the advice of a great sage. I was in a holding pattern in mid-2013 and I only wish this book would have been available then."

Dr. Mom, thank you for the honor of being asked to endorse this great book. May God bless it and use it to help his followers.

Ross Alan Hill,
Founder and CEO of Bank2, Oklahoma City, OK.

Dr. Herldleen Russell has written a wonderful book about what happens when we cease to be in control of our lives. Using the analogy of one who is stuck on an airline flight when that flight has been put in a holding pattern, she helps the reader reflect on what happens when our lives are in a holding pattern. She also helps the reader see holding patterns in our lives from a spiritual perspective. She postulates that when in the holding pattern, perhaps God has gone ahead of you and is preparing for your landing. She acknowledges the frustration of the loss of control, but encourages the reader to see the purpose of God for the holding pattern.

I, wholeheartedly, endorse Dr. Russell and the book that she has written. She is a gift to the body of Christ serving as Supervisor in the Church of God in Christ in both the Republic of Uganda and Greater Maryland First Jurisdictions. She has been creative in serving in the missions jurisdiction of the Republic of Uganda having taken on the hard tasks of educating pastors, planting schools, establishing orphanages, providing clean drinking water and evangelizing the lost. She has worked untiringly in Maryland supporting the approximately 50 local churches and leading women's ministries. Having traveled the length and breadth of the United States and the continent of Africa, she understands what it means to be in a "holding pattern." She also understands what it means to use that time to one's best advantage.

Dr. Russell's book would serve one well as devotional reading or as a gift to a friend who is "Between a Rock and a Hard Place."

Superintendent Tony W. Torain, M.A., M.S.W., M.Div., J.D.
Pastor – The Good Shepherd Church of God In Christ, Baltimore
Former Associate Dean – University of Baltimore School of Law
Interim Dean – C.H. Mason Jurisdictional Institute – Greater
Maryland First Jurisdiction

Herldleen Russell addresses clearly and concisely the critical questions often confronted by all individuals who seem to be at a standstill in reaching their goals in life. She compares the "Holding Pattern" maneuver of airplanes to the times in our lives when things are not moving in the direction we want to go. She uses scripture and experiences to give various strategies that will help one survive these seasons of inactivity.

Dr. Sheary D. Johnson,
Supervisor Virginia #4, Church Of God In Christ

Dr. Russell compels the reader to passionately but patiently seek God's purpose and promises by choosing the PERFECT WILL journey. Your book was my best and favorite 2013 read. Yes, I introspectively and graciously read it personally to yield a different and better result in 2014 and beyond. This was a great and inspiring read for me. I loved and definitely related to your flight analogies. In the midst of all the turbulence, you still manage to land safely and orchestrate favorable conditions even for the Community Day. What is beautiful to watch is your execution and awareness of your own Godly strength.

This book will certainly help people to better understand what drives your heart especially those who do not know already.

Michelle Gross,
Director of Admissions,
Coppin State University

A most inspiring and impactful encouragement for all! While life is filled with meantimes and periods of the state of marking time, it is good to know that God's intentions however remain sure. Easy is not the pathway to the destinies we are often prescribed in life, however we have the assurance that when our progress does not equate to the energy exerted in getting there, Heaven remains at work on our behalf and in our favor. Dr. Herldleen Russell echoes an insightful word for anyone that is twix and between the promise and the manifestation; the directive of God and the realization of it. An easy read, it addresses what the proper appropriation of the believer's behavior must be when standing in a critical context just outside the place He has directed and is taking one to. I recommend this book to every individual who feels stagnated and stunted by the deterrents of their destiny.

Carl A. Pierce, Sr.
Senior Pastor, Carter Memorial Church Of God in Christ
Baltimore, Maryland

During a time in the world when the economy is unstable, people are losing their homes, the government is sequestering, people are committing suicide people are beginning to question their faith. It is just like God to raise up a Dr. Herldleen Russell to speak to the very essence of our existence. Dr. Russell is spiritually qualified and also qualified in helping others to survive. She is affectionately known as Dr. Mom by the people of Uganda where she has provided resources for their survival when they found themselves "Between a Rock and Hard Place."

This book speaks to every facet of our lives. It not only speaks to our lives but it gives hope and explanation to the phases in our lives that we will encounter as long as we are on this terra firma

The Prophets of old spoke with faith and boldness when they heard a word from the Lord. This literary master piece gives hope to the hopeless, strength to the weak and helps us to build on the Rock. So when we come to the Hard Place Dr. Russell declares that we shall know the truth and the truth will help us to survive between the Rock and the Hard Place.

The readers of this book will never be the same because it will propel us to a deeper sense of being, a desire to survive and also a greater Love for God. Thank you Dr. Mom, Dr. Supervisor Russell for listening to God and sharing with His people.

ViCurtis Little, Pastor
Greater Deliverance Church of God in Christ
Supervisor
Washington, D.C. Jurisdiction

A Rock and A Hard Place masterfully depicts a place we have all found ourselves in at some point in our lives, wondering how we got there. It is refreshing to identify the stages: a holding pattern, promise to rest, prediction to prayer, and that the promise is manifested in the perseverance.

If you find yourself at a standstill or feel that you are not moving fast enough this book will shed light for your journey serving as a reminder that God is faithful and does cause us to walk by faith and not by sight!

Evangelist Brenda Johnson
Jesus Cares Ministries, Inc.

Praise for "Between a Rock and a Hard Place" This book is insightful, enlightening and scriptural. The trinity of writing for me. Dr. Russell has done a superior job with this erudite rendering. It helped me to understand (and tolerate) my valley experience! This is a must read for clergy and lay people. God bless you Dr. Russell. I've been inspired by your engaging prose to "hold on".

Elder Larry E. Flagg
Minister of Administration
Refreshing Spring COGIC

Acknowledgements

The many that encouraged me to write and patiently waited for me to complete this book. To Tawanda Davis, who pushed, and at times gently shoved me to go forward in my writing. You many times endured my procrastination, my changing edits and my endless schedule rearrangements, yet patiently endured until the completion of this book. Thank you.

TO GOD BE THE GLORY!

Dedication

I dedicate this book to my mother Bessie Lott, who first introduce me to Jesus Christ and was the example of how to live for Him and my personal intercessor. My husband, Herbert Jason Russell who has been my "rock"…for the past 44 years, in every hard place and my pastor. You have encouraged me to stand on The Rock, Jesus Christ, the living Word a sure foundation and to know and trust the Written Word… no matter what my eyes have shown me.

To my children…Cory, Karen, Terrence, Patrick, TeKesha, Stephanie, Rueben and Rachel, my 17 grandchildren and my precious Kennedy my first great-grand daughter. All of my sons and daughters both natural and spiritual. My church family, Ridgley Ministries Church of God in Christ and all of those who have prayed me through those hard places and encouraged me to remain in His "holding pattern"

Foreword

It is indeed an honor and privilege to have been given this opportunity to pen these words in reference to Dr. Herldleen Russell. Serving as General Supervisor of the Church of God in Christ Department of Women for the past sixteen years, I have come to know Dr. Russell personally.

Dr. Russell serves on the Department of Women Advisory Board. These women are selected and appointed by the General Supervisor because of their dedication, loyalty and are experienced in women's ministry. As such they are capable of giving wise counsel and advice for strengthening each phase of the work to the General Supervisor.

Dr. Russell's ministry has extended internationally in the Church of God in Christ in setting goals for the mission of the Women's Department; better homes, better families, better communities and a better World. My desire to afford a good Christian education to the orphans and children of Africa has been executed by Dr. Russell in the establishing of the Dr. Willie Mae Rivers Primary School in Uganda. This school will not only provide an education for these children but will serve as a proto-type to create an environment for training of teachers in surrounding areas to maximize their efforts in educating children in their schools

Her book exemplifies struggles, each of us at some point in our lives have experienced. We get seemingly "stuck" in non-progression towards our life goals. If you want to know how to handle being between that rock and hard place from a spiritual point of view this book is a must read! Within this book you will find how to handle being in a holding pattern even if you become frustrated, it leads you to a place of worship to revealing the promises in perseverance.

Everyone that read this book will be blessed. This literature will serve as a great tool; learning and discovering the value of standing still to see the salvation of the Lord!

Dr. Willie Mae Rivers
General Supervisor, Department of Women
Church of God in Christ, Inc.

CHAPTER 1

How Did I Get Here

· · · · · · · · · · · · · · · · ·

"Life happens to the best laid plans"

A *completed* journey is one in which a person has traveled from a starting point to an ending point. Sound simple? It would be, but life happens in between. In other words, life happens to the best-laid plans.

Imagine that you are on a flight after having rushed to have made it onto the plane on time. While you are settled into your seat, your mind hasn't simultaneously settled. Instead, your thoughts continue traveling to the things that are awaiting you at the end of your trip. You also anticipate the many things that need to be done. Your thoughts also turn to your accomplishments. You feel really good about your past strivings and are satisfied that you have achieved at least some of the things you had been hoping to do. The other matters, you just press past them, refusing to allow them to stop you. "Let's move forward no matter what" has been your response to everything that has tried to stop you or hold you back.

On the flight, you look at your watch: you are on time for landing. What relief you feel, knowing what kind of havoc a late flight can wreak on your schedule. Ah, you're almost at your destination.

Then comes an announcement from the captain: "We are experiencing some problems and are unable to land at this time, but we will land momentarily. I will keep you updated." When the captain announces the update, he or she uses these words: "We are in a holding pattern and can't move forward to land."

You thought that you were right on the verge of departing the plane and continuing on along your journey, so, certainly, you will not go back from where you came. You will just have to wait to move forward. It is then that the reality sets in: *I can't move forward.*

Is this a description of your life now? Do you feel like you are between a proverbial rock and a hard place—and that, as a result, your life has been placed on hold? Everything is moving ahead of you, but you are just running in place and marking time. And you just might be right about that. You might be in one of *God's holding patterns.*

The Rock and the Hard Place

And the Lord said to Moses, Speak to the children of Israel ... that they turn and encamp by the sea. For Pharaoh will say, they are entangled in the land, the wilderness hath shut them in. ... For the Egyptians pursued after them, all the horses and chariots of Ph

people, Fear r

of the Lord

Exodus 14: 1

The Lord wi

peace ... A

are you cry

of Israel, tl

rod, and st

divide it: ¿

dry ground through the midst of

14:14, 16 KJV)

Dr. Herldleen Russell

They, as well as we, were deli

represents a severe type of

bondage we were in wh

to go back to that p

want to go forw

if we walk u

thing from

In E

When the children of Israel, after four hundred years in bondage, were released by Pharaoh and led out of Egypt by Moses, they had a destination to reach: the Promised Land, God had provided for them. Subsequently, Pharaoh changed his mind about having granted freedom to the slaves and so sent his army to pursue the Israelites, capture them, and bring them back to Egypt. Determined to go forward, the Israelites found themselves faced with the impassable Red Sea. This was not a stream one could quickly wade through but a sea.

The Israelites found themselves in a place where they couldn't move; they could neither go back nor go forward. They were between a rock and a hard place. Because they were God's people, however, they were in just the right place for a miracle. And so Moses instructed them, "Stand still and see the Salvation of the Lord."

vered out of Egypt. For us, Egypt
bondage—slavery. We remember the
en we dwelled in sin. We have no desire
ace. We decidedly will not go back. We just
rd and into His promises. He has spoken that
right before Him, then He will withhold no good
us.

gypt, God proved himself to his weary children and delivered
em with His mighty hand, showing them miraculous signs and
wonders. It is no doubt that He is the God of miracles. What he
did for the Israelites at the Red Sea, He can do again.

When the Red Sea Does Not Open Up

What if the miracle is not happening in your life, though? If the
Red Sea is not opening up so that you may pass through this place
in your life and proceed toward the destination, your destiny, then
you are still between a rock and a hard place.

What makes it worse is that the Enemy seems to be gaining on
you. You can almost feel his breath on your neck. "What's with
this, God?" you ask. "I am still waiting for my miracle, the way
out of no way out." How often have I heard these sentiments
spoken by others! I have expressed them myself, time and time
again.

CHAPTER 2

Not a Rock and Hard Place: A Holding Pattern

· · · · · · · · · · · · · · · · ·

Then I heard Him speak: "*You are not between a rock and a hard place. I have you in a holding pattern—my holding pattern.*"

A holding pattern? I know what it means to be placed on hold—to endure a time of inactivation, waiting to be released so that I may continue what I had started. But a holding pattern? After God spoke to me, I dutifully googled the phrase *holding pattern* so as to learn the aeronautical definition.

What Is a Holding Pattern?

A holding pattern is a usual circular pattern flown by an aircraft when awaiting clearance to land at an airport. Though it is a state of waiting, it is a *pattern* flown in an oval shape, where the craft makes a series of 360-degree turns to avoid other aircrafts or to wait for clearance to land. Although a holding pattern is a fairly easy maneuver compared to other tasks in instrumentation flying, it's a source of confusion and apprehension. This is because a holding pattern is a state of waiting, one of suspended activity or progress.

Airplanes, when hoping to land, sometimes have to fly in a holding pattern because the *situation is not conducive for landing*. For example, there may be no gate or terminal ready for the plane to move into; the equipment to deplane may not be where it needs to be; the runway may be overcrowded; the area of travel may not be clear; there may be a storm; or another plane may be too close.

Now that we understand what a holding pattern is, we can begin to face the problems that arise when we find ourselves in one.

The Problem

On the plane, you, the passenger, cannot see anything that is going on in the cockpit. Only the pilot and the people in the air tower are aware of the prevailing conditions. It's the air traffic controllers in the tower who make the decision and then communicate it to the pilot to use a holding pattern until things are conducive for his or her landing. You yourself can't see or do anything to facilitate the plane's landing, so you just have to wait until everything is clear to land and the craft is ready to move forward.

The Holy Spirit School of Learning

God has my destiny (and my destination) already planned. *Life happens* in the execution of His plans, of which He is aware, but of which I am not.

On a flight, I cannot see much of what is happening in the cockpit or the air tower. It's up to the pilot and the air traffic controllers to orchestrate the next events. I realize this. I have to trust them, their expertise and experience, to deliver me safely to my destination. So it is with the Lord. We have to trust Him during this time, place, and season of our lives.

Knowing in your heart does not stop your emotions from taking over. Instead, you start your own pattern of thinking.

Thoughts We Have While in the Holding Pattern

I am losing precious time is a prevalent thought one might have while in one of God's holding patterns. When I look at my schedule, the things I have to accomplish and the deadlines that *I* have or someone else has instituted, I realize that I will *miss* my connecting flight or the person I am supposed to meet who is part of the plan for *my destination,* all because I'm sitting here waiting.

What is more evident than anything else is that I now have no control. No amount of my planning, influence, or expertise can help me out.

No Time Is Wasted When You Are Waiting on God
Here comes a truth. "The steps of a good man/woman are ordered by the Lord."(Psalm 37:23)….. He has it all under control.

Just because you can't see the pilot or the air tower commander does not mean that they are not working to bring you out of that pattern and lead you on to your destination, your destiny. It was in faith that you boarded the plane in the first place, because you trusted at the very beginning that the pilot and the air tower would chart and complete your journey.

Working the Pattern

You know that the people in the air tower and the pilot are not sitting idly by or taking a coffee break. The vessel is not aimlessly flying. It is actually flying a worked-out pattern. This pattern is charted. It's similar to the "eagle wings" of Isaiah 40, which are given to those who wait on the Lord. "They shall mount up with wings of eagles ... run and not be weary ... walk and not faint." (Isaiah 40:31 KJV) If I recognize that waiting is the Lord's plan for me, then I will see purpose in it, neither growing weary nor fainting.

The air traffic controllers' and the pilot's expertise are at work. You trust that. It's called *faith in things hoped for.* Just because you can't see them doesn't mean that they have forgotten that this is their job, one for which they have been trained and have the experience and expertise to accomplish. So much more should you trust the God who has *not* brought you this far only to leave you stranded. He is at work executing a preplanned pattern for your life so as to work everything out "for your good." This is called *evidence of things not seen.*

Now I recall one of my favorite passages of Scripture. God told His prophet to encourage his people in their season of weariness. They had thought God had forgotten about them. He sent this word: "Can a mother forget her suckling child?" (Isaiah 49:15 KJV) (Physically, this is a nearly impossible thing to do; just ask any nursing mother.) God says that a mother *may* forget her nursing child, but that He will not forget you, as He has written your name in the palm of His hand.

When Jeremiah was sent to the potter's house to see and learn what God wanted him to discover about what was going on in his life at that time, he found the potter making a vessel. After the vessel was finished, the potter examined it in his hand and found it to have flaws, so he took the time to make it over again (Jeremiah 18).

Similarly, God wants perfection in our lives. He does not want just any old vessel to function in just any kind of way. He wants a perfect vessel. You (the vessel) and your purpose will not be second rate; it will be the best.

In this passage of Scripture, it's important to note, when the potter is removing the flaws from it, that *the vessel is still in the potter's hand,* (Jeremiah 18KJV) safe and secure. Jesus said, "No man can pluck you out of His hand" (John 10:28–29 KJV). He is still in control. Jumping out of His hand by making your own decisions is as foolish as jumping out of the plane that is flying in a holding pattern. Your attempt to fast-forward time to get to where you want to be will result in your splattering on the ground.

Time is not lost during these times; on the contrary, it's being used to perfect you. The pilot, the mechanic (if necessary), and the air traffic controllers are working it all out to bring you to that "expected end," as noted by Jeremiah, the prophet. Picture the Godhead at work just for you.

Let's return to our scenario aboard the aircraft. While we're waiting to land, we receive another update. The pilot says, "There are too many on the runway for us to land. We can't get to our assigned gate, as another plane is currently at that gate." *Some other plane is in the way.*

Timing and Positioning

You may grumble to yourself when confronted with the prospect of something's or someone's being ahead of you, "This is just in my way, keeping me from completing what I need to do." Therefore, your thoughts become self-centered and possessive: *Those other people's time is up; they must move away from* my gate *so I can move in and go forward.*

Did You Ever Think of This?

Just *maybe* those ahead of you are *making the way* for you. Is it possible that they are fulfilling their ministry so you can take your own ministry to the next level?

Other things and people are not *in the way,* although it appears that they are occupying what you consider to be your space. God has ordained this space in time for another person, so that he or she may perhaps provide counseling, a role model, an example you need, etc. Another may be laying a path for you so that you can walk over it much more easily, thereby enabling you to complete your journey.

As we are the body fitly joined together, we work to each other's benefit, whether we are aware of it or not. Therefore, "Seeing that we are compassed about with so great a cloud of witnesses ... let us run the race with patience" (Hebrews 12:1).

The fact is that you just might not be ready to move onto the next step, or it might not yet be time for you to occupy that particular space. *Know* when it is your season. You may feel it's your season of harvest however, it might now be.. Just as important as knowing when it is your season is knowing when your time or season is over. When you know your job is done, then you can freely move onto the next task.

When it is not Time to move on to the next task. that word of itself is so frustrating to me. And I feel frustration acutely now because more time has passed. I'm not understanding I now sit in my *seat of frustration,* waiting on God.. Asking this question, God what time will you move me from this place.

My mind goes back to Exodus, when the children of Israel were almost to the Red Sea and the thunder of horses' hoofs from Pharaoh's army were getting nearer and nearer, louder and louder. You know that their purpose was to overtake the Israelites and consume and destroy all their future endeavors, thereby also destroying their destiny.

When you are in this type of situation, you think, *This is going to be a great setback to my plans—for only God knows how long.* Yet as you sit in the seat of frustration, you are constantly trying to be the good witness, the example of faith. But the sound of the Enemy is drowning out the sound of that word of promise—the goal you are trying to reach. You begin to hear, just as Moses heard, other people's complaints escalating, multiplying. If you are in an aircraft that is flying in a holding pattern, you now hear the complaining voices of other passengers more loudly than you hear His voice of promise and direction.

Remember the description of how some pilots feel about flying in a holding pattern: for them, it is "a source of confusion and apprehension, a state of waiting or suspended activity." Sometimes for us that same door opens—and through it walks those negative emotions that we allow ourselves to feel.

CHAPTER 3

Frustrations in the *Holding Pattern*

· · · · · · · · · · · · · · · ·

All of a sudden, we may find ourselves having feelings of being *abused.* Because I can't go anywhere, I can be treated in any kind of way. I'm totally at the mercy of those I can't see. "What about the flight attendants" (who are among those I *can* see)? "They are not really helping at this point. They can't answer my questions. My attendant is running out of peanuts and pretzels and juice. She is just a body that is *supposed* to be of comfort in these types of situations, but she is prevented from serving me as I'd like because of the limitations inherent in the holding pattern. The attendants are just staying in their lanes to fulfill their responsibilities. But I have determined that they should know more than they are in a place to know. I am looking to them to do what they have not been trained to do. However, even though they *know the problem,* they *don't have the solution.*

Have I started looking to someone else for solutions and answers that only the pilot and the air traffic controller can give, as they are the ones who orchestrate the journey? These are the ones who issue directives in *perfect time.*

Now, if I'm not careful, I start venting my anger on those who are assisting and attempting to make this part of my journey easier while I'm waiting. If I don't check myself, then I start having *feelings of rejection.* I am ringing my caller bell because I am looking to someone who I think *should* know what's going on, but the assistants *don't* know. They are starting to ignore me because what can they tell me other than what the pilot has announced? They are not the ones who have planned the journey and are preordained to take me to its "expected end." I am wasting my time in seeking answers from those who do not have them.

From Abiding in a Holding Pattern to Being "Stuck"

Too much time has now passed, we might think aboard the plane. *We should have been moving by now.* At this point in time, we may experience emotional extremes: *What if I am just stuck in this "black hole" of time from which I will never get free, doomed to circle and circle until …?*

If I go back and reflect on the children of Israel and remember their journey in the wilderness, I see that they remained inside a holding pattern for a very long time. Even though they were moving, they were not getting anywhere soon, as they wandered in the desert for forty years. Their course of travel may not have been a circular one, but it did require a great deal of waiting and patience nonetheless.

God told Moses in the midst of the exodus that these, His people, needed a *place of worship.* He instructed Moses to build a tabernacle.

Why worship? Oh, we know that it's important, but we just want to reach our destination, the *Promised Land.* Building a tabernacle, it seems, will take *more time* away from the charted journey.

Worship in the Time of Your Holding Pattern

God gives explicit instructions for the Israelites to construct the tabernacle (which is, in essence, a movable church). Even though it was to be portable, God still instructed them to take and use the very best materials in its preparation: fine gold and linen draperies. The ark of the covenant, which represents the presence of God, was very detailed in its construction.

The message is this: *Take time to worship,* no matter where you are, even if you are between a rock and a hard place in the wilderness and can't see the way ahead. Take time to worship. Don't just give a shoddy cry of, "Get me out of here!"—but engage in real worship. Get into the presence of God; give him your best.

As David said in Psalm 27:4 KJV, to worship is "To behold the beauty of the Lord and to inquire in his Temple." "Refresh yourself in God's Word," is the gist of what David the psalmist said. There were things. "" I did not understand until I went into the sanctuary, in His presence, and then I *understood* the end. Psalm 73:17

One of the outstanding events that happened on the day when Jesus died at Calvary was the vail in Jerusalem's temple was torn from top to bottom. The book of Hebrews records the purpose for this. Prior to Jesus' crucifixion and resurrection, only a high priest was privileged to go into the "holiest of holy places" to speak directly to God. We now have direct access to the throne room, however. We can boldly approach the throne of grace, from where we may receive God's help in our time of need.

We have direct access to His presence. Let us use it.

The whole beautifully constructed tabernacle had to be portable because Moses and the Israelites were traveling. When they were instructed to move on, they had to take down the tabernacle and move it, only to put it back up when they reached a place where God told them to stop. The tabernacle had to be portable because the Israelites did not stay in any one place for long.

We can be edified by their experience. Though our frustrations would have us feel stuck, we are assured that they are not here to stay.

At some point, I imagine, the wanderers in the desert started to feel that their nomadic way of life would go on forever, that it was just going to be a part of their existence. Treadmills did not exist at that time, obviously, but if they had, then surely some of the Israelites would have likened their wanderings to being on a treadmill: Stop; put up the tabernacle; worship; break down the tabernacle; move out. Stop; assemble the tabernacle; worship God; break it down; move out. Surely, some of them felt *stuck in the procedure* and thought, *So will go our lives. Will we ever make it to the place of promise, or will we do this for the rest of our lives?* I imagine that you, too, have had thoughts like these.

There is a very dangerous component to being stuck. When it stretches beyond merely remaining in a certain place for a designated period of time, the holding place can become a place of darkness, so dark that the Enemy can make you believe that it is now a place that you will *never* get out of, thereby laying the groundwork for you to enter into depression. Depression is that "dark hole" of seemingly no escape—a sinkhole.

As I was writing the above paragraph, I heard the news that the son of a very popular person in ministry, a renowned pastor, had just committed suicide. He said that his son was unable to "shake the darkness" that had so surrounded him. His pain had become so great that the only way to escape the place he had entered into and to stop the pain was—or so he thought—to take his own life.

The Devil is a robber of all that is good. The Bible says, "The thief comes to steal, kill and destroy. Jesus said, 'I have come that you might have life and that life more abundantly'" (John 10:10). He gave His life for you so you can live a life of abundance.

Stop listening to the lies of the Enemy, and start speaking the Word of God over your life and believing what God says about you. Watch your *attitude* when you become frustrated. Frustration and a bad attitude can lead to your doubting God. If you already feel stuck in a place, then doubting God can lead you to feel hopeless. You may become miserable in the holding pattern.

CHAPTER 4

Where do I Go... when I can't Move

· · · · · · · · · · · · · · · ·

Moving to... the place of Promise

I move and position myself in the place where He has made promises and I am assured of his working things out. Moving to the place of promise, however, requires *patience,* not doubt. "Patience," said the Bible teacher Martin De Haan II, "is not a desperate waiting in doubt, but a hopeful waiting in confidence"— not on those who are around and a part of the process, but on the Lord.

King Jehoshaphat, as recorded in 2 Chronicles 20, saw that he and God's people were surrounded by their enemy. Indeed, they were outnumbered, without the slightest hope of victory. Jehoshaphat recognized that he had to stop and immediately take his eyes off the present circumstances, the evidence he saw in his environment. Then he said to God, "Our eyes are upon thee."

One day I was so tired and cried out, "Lord, my eyes are upon you." And I heard the Lord say, "Be not weary in well doing; you will reap *if* you faint not." *Well doing* seemed to be a key here, so I began to dig a little deeper in my prayers because I wanted to make sure I was *doing well* when I was *doing what* He wanted me to do.

I prayed again, and He spoke to me from 1 Corinthians 15:58: "Be ye steadfast, unmovable, always abounding in the work of the Lord, knowing your labor is not in vain in the Lord."

Steadfast. Isn't that what Moses told his people to be? The message to them and me alike was to stand still—not to be immobile, but still, so as to *see* the salvation of the Lord. And then the Scripture uses the word *unmovable.* I take that to mean, "Don't move from where you are. Stand still with expectation."

While you are standing still with expectation, you are building a foundation for being steadfast. *I'm not going to move because God is getting ready to,* should be what you're thinking. But the Lord also wants you to know that your work for Him is never in vain. Put your focus back on Him. "Those that wait on the Lord shall not be ashamed." "(Psalms 25:2,3 What a revelation! We should not be waiting for the circumstance to improve or change; we should be *waiting on the Lord.*

Oh my, here is an occasion to use the word that always seem to follow the word *wait: patience.* You have need of patience, as do I. The book of Hebrews speaks again: "You have need of Patience after you have done the will of God you will receive the promise". Hebrews 10:36

When you can't move, you must know that God is in charge and that He is working out something in you and for you. He is always at work. That plane is flying a *distinct pattern* during its waiting time. We should be doing the same.

Have you ever thought that God might just be trying to get your attention? He usually does get our attention when we lose all control over a situation.

This Is a Time to Review and Reflect

Ask yourself the following: In my haste to make it to my destination on time, have I skipped something that God wanted me to do? Have I bypassed something that is the *will of God* and which I must accomplish before moving ahead?

We so often forget—in seeing and moving in our purpose—to pray that the will of God be done. It is what Jesus taught his disciples in the "model" prayer: "Thy will be done on earth as it is in heaven" (Matthew 6:10).

However, we must still be cautious. The excitement of our accomplishments can move us from the "perfect will of God" into "permissive will."

Remembering Balaam and Balak (Numbers 22–24)

While the children of Israel were journeying to the Promised Land, they passed through Moab, near Jordan. Balak was King of the Moabites. The Israelites were great in number, and Balak knew that his forces could not easily wipe them out. He sent for the prophet Balaam. He thought that the only way his kingdom could survive their assault or their passing through was for the prophet to curse them. So he sent a message to the prophet (with an offering, of course) asking him to do just that.

The prophet Balaam responded and said that he needed to first talk to the Lord about King Balak's request. God responded to Balaam, "You will not go back to King Balak, nor will you curse the people of Israel, for they are blessed" Numbers 22:12.

King Balak sent word again to Balaam, offering him a promotion of great honor. Balaam sent these words back to Balak: "If you offer me your house full of silver and gold, I cannot go beyond the Word of the Lord my God to do less or more. But I will ask again. Numbers 22: 18

Why would Balaam ask again when God was emphatic about Balaam's having nothing to do with King Balak because the king wanted Balaam to curse God's people?

God's perfect will was that his prophet not even be among the Moabites (or their king) because of the influence they could wield over him to disobey God.

Still, Balaam asked again. And this time, God gave him permission, His permissive will, to go. As the Bible story continues, we learn that God was angry at the prophet for pursuing this journey. On his way, an angel of the Lord stood in his path with his sword drawn. The donkey that Balaam was riding saw the angel and ran the other way. Balaam did not see the angel and began hitting the donkey to make him obey, which is ironic because Balaam did not immediately obey his God. Balaam the prophet should have been the one to have seen the angel; instead, his donkey did. That Balaam wanted to kill his donkey with the angel's sword is another instance of irony, as it is Balaam's life that is threatened by the sword of the angel. Balaam's prophetic insight had been dimmed by the prospect of an earthly reward.

Seeking rewards such as money, position, and power can blind you and move you out of God's will for your life.

We want to be in the perfect will of God. We never want to try to force the hand of God for our own selfish benefit. We never want him to say to us after, our continuous begging to have it our way, "Just go ahead and do it, and suffer the dire consequences later." Out of the will of God is a terrible place to be. In the will of God is a place of peace and safety.

It's the "Yes, Lord" to His *will* and the "Yes, Lord" to His *ways* of accomplishing His will that allows us consistently to surrender and ensure that our will and methods do not overshadow His. In other words, make sure you're doing things His way. For it is after, as Hebrews says, "you have done the will of God … [that] you will *receive* the promise" (Hebrews 10:36emphasis added).

It is easy to become frustrated, though. Some of the greatest patriarchs of the Bible found themselves in a state of frustration. This happens usually when our desires and anticipations overshadow and move to suppress the perfect timing of the will of God. That's when we become *impatient.* And if we do not check our impatience, then it leads us to *doubt*—our doubting the God whom we are to trust in every circumstance. Doubt is a seed planted into what was supposed to be a flower bed blooming with the promises of God, and which now becomes a bed of frustration with weeds of *hopelessness* popping up and choking out those promises. Doubt is a bed whereupon you want to lie down and cry.

Are you sensing a feeling of hopelessness? I want you to know that it is but another experience in the holding pattern.

When Anticipation Moves into Hopelessness

Let's look at some people who were dear to Jesus and who found themselves in a place of doubt and hopelessness: Mary, Martha, and Lazarus. Mary was a worshiper; Martha, a worker; and Lazarus, a friend. Each one of these people experienced a relationship with Jesus. Jesus called them His friends. Martha enjoyed preparing dinners for Jesus and his disciples when they were in town. Mary sat at his feet with no other desire than to hear his words. That, to her, was a need "more than [her] necessary food" (Job 23:12). Much to Martha's dismay, Mary also worshiped at Jesus' feet, giving her all. Each had a unique relationship with Jesus—a "needful" one, as He once said at their house. They were a family who loved Jesus and expressed it.

As life happens to the best-laid plans, however, Lazarus got sick.

Of course, Mary and Martha sent for Jesus. Now the Bible emphatically states, "Jesus loved Mary, Martha and Lazarus" John 11:3 ; however, He waited two or more days *after* he received news of Lazarus' sickness to begin traveling to their home in Judea.

Can you imagine Mary and Martha pacing endlessly back and forth, waiting for Jesus to arrive at any moment? They were in a holding pattern. They were not yet at a moment of frustration. Initially, they lived in expectation and anticipation because they, Jesus' friends, whom He loved, believed He would soon come. After Jesus did not appear, Mary and Martha's life entered into a holding pattern, and they became filled with anxiety, impatience, and frustration. When Lazarus died, their hope, dreams, and anticipation ended.

Our waiting for our Lord and friend was in vain and hopeless, they might have thought.

Jesus' timing, however, is always perfect even when it *seems* too late. He knows what He is doing by placing people in a holding pattern.

The *purpose* of Mary and Martha's holding pattern was greater than they could ever have anticipated. Jesus would bring more than just healing; He would deliver a miraculous breakthrough. Death, the last unconquered enemy, would be defeated, and an astounding revelation would be spoken and revealed: "I am the resurrection and the life. He that believes in me though He were dead. Yet shall he live John 11:25."

We would never again have to fear death. He proved Himself to be Lord of all. The grave had to give up Lazarus at the sound of the voice of life Himself, Jesus. Death would no longer have a sting; the grave would no longer be the victor.

And Jesus used Mary and Martha, His friends whom He loved, as witnesses to and receivers of His gift.

Are you His friend? He loves you. Will you trust Him with the results?

What Is the Holding Pattern God Has You In?

Take a moment to write down the holding pattern in which you find yourself. It could be an illness, an anticipated promotion, a promised position, or another promise given you. You were seemingly on the verge of receipt of healing or of something else grand, but now you are experiencing a delay—or, perhaps, what you were promised and had anticipated was recently given to someone else instead.

A promise broken. Where do we go from here? For me, my "flight" becomes one of getting away when my hopes are dashed. How do you cope with broken promises and dashed hopes? Take the time to write that down, as well.

Giants We Face While in the Holding Pattern

Giants are those oversize, overwhelming things that we see overshadowing everything and becoming larger than *the promise* we were given. Giants push back the possibility of that promise's being realized, drowning it in a sea of doubt and discouragement. And it now no longer appears to be God's holding pattern we're abiding in, but rather a serious problem that demands we take some kind of action.

I have noticed that several things can happen when giants show up in our lives. Giants, because of their size, speak louder than any person and soon become intimidating. Following are the giant voices we may hear during this time.

The Giant of Complaint

We may make or hear complaints about what could be, what should be. Remember Moses and the people at the Red Sea? They held Moses responsible—playing the blame game. Speaking loudly, their complaining soon drowned out what God had promised them.

On the airplane, you start listening to those around you. That person sitting next to you is complaining, and you eventually join in. Complaining causes you to take your eyes off your purpose, the promise, and your destination.

The Giant of Ingratitude

You feel unappreciated after doing all that you could. You ask yourself how you are supposed to encourage others when you need encouragement yourself. How can you have an attitude of gratitude in the middle of all this complaining, which is slowly chipping away at the foundation of your positive thinking and good attitude? Still, you are constantly trying to be the good witness, the example of faith.

Sometimes I get really scared myself, but I can't let those who have trusted in my call and my ministry sees me waver and lose faith. My refrain becomes, "Never let them see you sweat" (remember that television commercial?).

What did Moses do when he was between a rock and a hard place and those "giants" showed up? He spoke a word of confidence into the situation and to counter the voices that were speaking discouragement and defeat.

We are reminded again: stand still. Yes, stand still. You can't go forward; it's out of your control. Stand still, not out of fear or exasperation and because you can't do anything else (land a plane, move the obstacles that prevent landing), but because you are willing to stand still *in anticipation* and *expectation, confident* and *undismayed,* so as to "see the salvation of the Lord." Here is the Word from the Lord:

"For the Egyptians you have seen today you shall never see again Exodus 14:13."

In other words, you are learning a great lesson. Once through it, you won't ever have to pass this way again.

Don't even worry about your obstacles: the cause, the purpose robber, the confidence crusher, the destiny destroyer. Why? Because the Lord will fight for you, and you shall hold your peace and remain at rest (Exodus 14:13–14).

Know that you are simply abiding in His holding pattern, whereby you will come to experience your miracle-working God who will not allow time, the elements, physical barriers, or emotional concerns stop Him from completing His plan for your life.

The holding pattern you are in must lead you to stop and refocus on Him, the author and finisher of your faith (Hebrews 12:2).

By faith you *accepted* the work that He completed by dying on the cross for you. By grace you are saved through faith. It is the greatest miracle ever. So, can he not see you through this minor interruption? By faith you started this journey with Him, with the admonition to "run this race with patience Hebrews 12:1." Keep your focus on Him, and He will certainly complete what He began, as He is the finisher.

Your journey will have detours or what appear to be setbacks. It seems, sometimes, that you're losing ground—climbing two steps up the ladder only to take four steps back. Setback after setback interrupts you. Do you feel that?

Here the Lord speaks expressively to me. ***"Your comeback will be greater than your setback."***

Where Faith Comes In
"Now Faith is the substance of things hoped for and the evidence of things not seen" (Hebrews 11:1). Are you going to trust Him *for evidence* (you *are* going to land, arrive at your destination, and complete your destiny, even though you cannot see it now)?

There is *evidence* that you cannot see, so you have to trust that God is at work. Even though you can't see His hand, you entrust the outcome of your journey to His heart.

You want to please Him. Don't forget that this is the ultimate goal of your life: that you please God. This means honoring His timetable, His schedule, and His methods. You are in a holding pattern to achieve the ultimate purpose: His will for your life. And remember that His way of achieving it is far better than any of *your* plans. Many are the plans of man, but it's God's purpose that prevails" (Isaiah 14;24.

We talk about stepping out in faith, which usually means *moving forward, taking the plunge,* as Peter did when he walked on water. But the ultimate trust is demonstrated when you can't move, and so you *rest* in Him, trusting in the *dark* what He previously revealed to you in the *light,* knowing that He is still working it out for you. This faith is substantial, the "substance of things hoped for."

CHAPTER 5

From **The Place of Promise to** *Rest*

. . . .

"For we who have believed, entered into that rest" *Hebrews 4:3*

The need to rest in Him, when you are in a *Holding Pattern.*

Ah, an idea: I'll just go to sleep and hope that when I wake up, everything will be all right and in place. When my eyes open, we will be moving into the gate so I can soon depart this plane.

Note well: *Sleep and rest are not the same things.*

Physically, you can sleep many hours and wake up feeling unrested. Emotionally, you can use sleep as an temporary escape from a problem. So, you must learn how to *rest* in God instead of becoming overtired and merely sleeping through the important parts of your life.

How Do I Rest?
Psalm 16:9 tells us, "Rest in hope." Biblical hope is not merely having an optimistic outlook or beholding the product of wishful

thinking without any foundation, but it is the sense of confident expectation based on solid certainty: a person. Hope's name is Jesus Christ.

Psalm 42 is a record of David's words when he was going through his go-through. He was experiencing a sense of despair and hopelessness. It was an unrest of such magnitude that it disturbed his spirit. His emotions took over, producing unrest. He described his soul as "disquieted within me" Psalms 42:5. When we feel this way, the desires of the flesh take over, which escalates the situation.

David had to shake himself. Sometimes you have to shake yourself to bring yourself back to the Word and what you know about God.

Paul said, "That I may know him ... in the power of His resurrection and the fellowship of his suffering" (Philippians 3:10). Every trial, every discouragement, and every disappointment would give Paul an opportunity to know Jesus better—not just learn more things about him, but *know Him,* have a more intimate relationship with Him.

Once you have the experience of knowing Jesus, it is something that no one can take away from you. It is deposited in *your knower,* as I like to say. This is when you know that you know that you know that you know. Daniel wrote, "Those that know their God shall be strong and do exploits Daniel 11:32."

Look at the steps David took, as described in Psalm 42. David examined himself. He questioned himself, not God. "Why art thou cast down, Oh my soul inner self and be disquiet within me

Psalm 42:5." He challenged his emotion by holding it up against the light of the Word of God.

Why am I feeling like this? He was asking. *What profit to my spirit and my walk with the Lord is this emotion? Rest* had left him; peace was following behind; and hopelessness was trying to *take root and thereby uproot* his hope and confidence. He put hope into action when he cried out, admonishing himself, "Hope thou in God Psalm 42:5." He considered that he may not have been moving as he had expected to the place he thought he would have reached by now. But with confident expectation based on the solid certainty of the promises of God, the God who cannot lie, David concluded, *I will.*

The book of Hebrews speaks again. "There remaineth a rest for the people of God Hebrews 4:9." But the Hebrew people did not attain rest because of their *doubt and unbelief.* But we can rest in hope and wait patiently for Him, as Psalm 37 makes clear.

Trouble Is Nothing New

God's people have always had problems with restlessness and anxiety, and as a result they took situations into their own hands and tried to work out the problem themselves, using their own methods and trusting in their own powers, not those of God. Doing so always results in a withdrawal of the rest and confidence found only in God, the God who would otherwise fight their battles and assure them of victory.

Isaiah 30:15 records the Lord's instructions and His rebuke during one of these times in His people's history. "For thus saith the Lord

God, the Holy One of Israel, 'In returning and rest shall you be saved in quietness and confidence shall be your strength and ye would not.'" How sad! Everything they needed to get through their crisis was available to them, and yet they chose not to use it ("and you would not").

God's Rest

God rested on the seventh day of creation. He rested not because He was tired, but because His work was completed. You and I can *rest* in the promises of God no matter what our problem is, because the work is completed. We cannot see it now, but it is already done. We enter into this rest of confidence wherein we can relax and receive the quiet assurance that God has got it all under control.

Bishop Charles E. Blake, the Presiding Bishop of The Church of God in Christ, told a story about a flight he was on. The aircraft entered into turbulence that rocked the plane. Things did not look good. Others on the plane were panicking, and rightly so. But Bishop Blake reminded the Lord of the work He had given him to do and that it was not yet finished; the plane *could not go down,* he was sure, so he just laid back and went to sleep. Now that is an example of entering into His rest. That is an example of resting in the God who has promised you and who orders your steps. Needless to say, the plane landed safely and Bishop Blake continued his journey.

He is our resting place, and when we rest in Him, we are strengthened by Him to accomplish the fullness of our destiny!

When the Holding Pattern Becomes a Desolate Place

You look out the window of the plane and see nothing, absolutely nothing. Maybe a few clouds; maybe not. What a place of desolation.

What Do You Do in Your Desolate Place?

And the apostles gathered themselves together unto Jesus, and told them all things, both what they had done, and what they had taught. And he said unto them. Come yourselves apart into a *desert place,* and rest a while for there were many coming and going and they had not leisure so much as to eat.

And they departed into a desert place by ship privately. And the people saw them departing and many knew him and ran afoot thither out of all cities, and out went them, and came together unto him. And Jesus, when he came out, saw much people and was moved with compassion toward them, because they were as sheep not having a shepherd: and he began to teach them many things ... And when the day was now far spent, his disciples came to him and said, *This is a desert place,* and now the time is far passed: Send them away that they may go into the country round about, and into the villages, and buy themselves bread: for they have nothing to eat Jesus said Give them to eat. (Mark 6:30–36, emphasis added)

First, it's interesting to note what we think of as a desolate place. Also interesting is that the place we choose to get away to is, most of the time, noisy and crowded, because it's usually the popular place. We ourselves will never choose, most of the time, to be in a desolate or deserted place.

In the passage of Scripture above, Jesus saw the people's *need* and therefore told them *what to do* and *where to go*.

The disciples had just experienced the worst possible thing in their lives and in their ministry. John, the popular speaker, crowd gatherer, baptizer, and forerunner of Christ, had just been executed simply for telling the truth. The disciples had gone and picked up his beheaded body and buried it. No doubt, thoughts ran through their minds: *If it happened to him, then it can certainly happen to us. We have been doing the best we can, doing everything that we thought right according to the plan and the purpose of God for our lives, with blessings following. Why and how did this happen? What do I do?* The first thing they did was run and tell Jesus, which is the smartest thing they could have done.

Whom do you tell when tragedy happens? I just got an email from a friend I've had for almost forty years. . She called me immediately to tell me of her pain. Her sister's grandson had just been found dead near their home No parent ever thinks that he or she will outlive his or her children—and certainly not his or her grandchildren. Though it is wonderful to have a friend, to reach out to immediately, how much greater to tell the one that understands AND..can respond to heal, comfort and encourage.

The doctor has ordered you to go for test..and you await the results, . The test results are in and a prognosis has been made. You reach for your phone. When problems arise, what is the first thing you do? Who is the person you call?

Here I am reminded of two of my favorite songs. The first is "I Must Tell Jesus": "I must tell Jesus all of my sorrows, / I cannot bear these burdens alone. / Jesus *can* help me, / Jesus *alone*" (emphasis added).

The second is "What a Friend We Have in Jesus":

> All our sins and grief to bear.
> What a privilege to carry everything
> To God in prayer. [Here comes the warning.]
> O what peace we often forfeit.
> O what needless pain we bear,
> All because we do not carry everything
> To God in prayer.

It is wonderful how He will, as David said, "Give you songs in [your] night [season] Psalm 77:6."

The Bible says that the apostles gathered themselves unto Jesus and told him what was going on. Jesus' reply was, "Come ye yourselves apart … into a desolate place … and rest a while Mark 6:31."

In your busyness, sometimes you just need to *rest* in the Lord. The Lord causes situations, places, and holding patterns in your life, so you must first rest, and then you'll be able to hear Him clearly.

Jesus knows your needs even if sometimes you don't. He'll allow you to enter into His promise or else send you to a *desert place* so that you may recollect yourself in Him before proceeding.

Now, the disciples' rest was very short-lived because they had to resume their ministry almost immediately. The Bible says, "The multitude appeared, running on foot out of all the cities Mark 6:33."

Jesus *never said* that He had sent them on vacation because they had been so busy. No, instead Jesus thought that His disciples had just experienced a tragedy, and so He advised them to "slip out" for a bit and rest. The passage of Scripture goes on to say, "He was moved with compassion toward them and taught them [the multitude] many things Mark 6:34."

Lesson: Be prepared to minister to others in your desolate place.

God allows things to come into your life to increase your experience and to use you later in light of those experiences. Because the most effective person is one who has experienced difficult things. The Lord allows you to go through trying times so that you might thereby relate to others to whom you minister who are going through similar things. It births in you compassion for others. Because you have been through that experience, and God has delivered you from it..you will become better able to speak positive words to your "seat mates on the airplane of life" during your holding pattern.

A person without compassion is a person who might have been called. But with lack of compassion has a dry and ineffective ministry.

The disciples recognized that that they were in a desert place, but they had been looking at it *negatively* instead of looking at it according to its *purpose*. And just what was its purpose? First, the disciples were to remove themselves from the crowd to be alone with Jesus. Next came the opportunity for them to minister to the multitudes. Last, they discovered this place to be a *place of miracles*.

However, the disciples, like we do, had looked solely at the natural environment and deemed it desolate; therefore, they could not see the purpose for which God had brought them to that *desolate place*. They also saw the crowd of hungry people, noting that there was no source of food. In this, they were overwhelmed by the misery and so missed the potential for a miracle, which is a transcendence of the natural environment.

How easily we can miss what God has in store for us! Here was Jesus, the Bread of Life, beside His disciples, but they could not even see the source of everything they needed because their focus was on the desert place.

They said, "*This is a desert place and now the time is far passed they are hungry send them away so that they can get something to eat Mark 6: 36.*"

They were looking with their natural eyes at the circumstance, and therefore they were blinded to the fact that Jesus was with them. *Never forget* that Jesus is with you in your desert place and in your holding pattern. Again, David the psalmist says, "You are my hiding place; you will protect me from trouble and surround me with songs of deliverance" (Psalm 32:7 NIV).

See It as Jesus Sees It

Jesus was able to look beyond the problem and see possibilities in a seemingly impossible situation. In faith, which is the *evidence of things not seen,* He said, "Feed them."

If Jesus says it, then it can be done. Find your promise in the Word, and know that if Jesus said it, then it can be done for you, too.

The disciples, however, went back to the natural again. They asked Jesus, "Should we go and buy 200 penny worth of bread?" Mark 6: 37

The fact is this: Jesus will supply whatever you need, right where you are and according to what you have there. Little becomes much in the Master's hand. He took a little boy's small lunch. What was the first thing He did with it? What He did with those loaves and fishes is what He'll do for you in your place of desolation.

Be thankful for what you have, because things could be worse. Stop complaining. Know that he is Jehovah Yireh, the Lord and your provider.

You know what happened next. Jesus took that little boy's lunch, the bread and the fish, and gave thanks. After He made this prayer of thanksgiving, He miraculously met the people's need in that place of desolation.

You must pray in your holding pattern. Take the time when the prediction is made, nothing to eat and the possibilities announced...no where to go and get what is needed because you are in a place of desolation. **Take *time* to Pray**

CHAPTER 6

From Prediction to Prayer

· · · · · · · · · · · · · · · · ·

When you are in a holding pattern, prayer is your lifeline. Notice that I didn't title this chapter "From Prediction to Fulfillment" or "From Prediction to Promise." No, I called it "From Prediction to Prayer."

When we hear the word *prediction,* most of us think of the weather. Flights have been canceled because of weather storms, and rightly so. No one wants to be caught in a bad storm while flying.

What happens to our plans and purposes when the storms of life happen?

We all love to pray for sunny days. We pray that the *sun* and the *Son* will shine every day so that we may enjoy nothing but great days. But we know that's not life.

I remember that our church was to hold its Community Day on a Saturday. The weather prediction was for rain and thunderstorms all day Saturday. In fact, as a precursor, it had rained for ten straight days prior to Community Day.

People began to speak of postponement. It had rained all week and was supposed to rain again. Our pastor said, "No, we will wait. And we are going to pray like Esther. I sent out a prayer alert to all the men and women."

When Community Day arrived, the predicted rain fell in the early morning. It was, in fact, accompanied by thunderstorms. I received a call early that morning from a person who told me that thundershowers were supposed to start at noon, the exact time when Community Day was supposed to begin. "Do you think we should cancel?" the person asked me.

"No, we are praying," I replied….. From prediction to prayer.

It was then I was reminded of the prophet Elijah in James 5:

> Is any among you afflicted? Let him pray. Is any merry? Let him sing psalms. Is any sick among you? Let him call for the elders of the church; and let them pray over him, anointing him with oil in the name of the Lord. And the prayer of faith shall save the sick, and the Lord shall raise him up; and if he have committed sins, they shall be forgiven him. … The effectual fervent prayer of a righteous man availeth much.
>
> Elias [Elijah] was a man subject to like passions as we are, and he prayed earnestly that it might not rain: and it rained not on the earth by the space of three years and six months. And he prayed again,

and the heaven gave rain, and the earth brought
forth her fruit. (James 5:13–18)

Elijah prayed, and as a result there was no rain for three and a half
years. Then he prayed again, and it rained after the drought that
had endured for more than three years.

First Kings 17:1 records this event and the exact words of Elijah:
"As the Lord God of Israel liveth, there shall not be dew nor rain
these years, but according to my word or except at my word." And
it did not rain during that time.

It is important to know that God took care of his servant Elijah
during this time. God will do the same for us. When we experience
a drought in our own lives, our assurance is that the righteous will
never be forsaken.

Let us remember how the widow fed Elijah in 1 Kings 17:8–16.
Elijah had been instructed to go to see her, as she would feed him.
There was a problem, however: all she had was a handful of meal
and a little oil. She was preparing to fix a little cake for her and
her son to eat, and then they would die. These were her words and
her prediction. But Elijah told her to go and do that, but to make
him a cake *first* before making one for her and her son.

First Fruits

Jesus said, "Seek Ye first the Kingdom of God and his righteousness
and all of these things [food, clothing, etc.] will be *added* unto
you" (emphasis Matthew 6:33 added).

Was Elijah being selfish when he requested that the widow feed him before feeding herself and her son? Was he, as people typically say of their preachers, only thinking about himself?

God often told His people to give Him the *first* of things on the altar of sacrifice. So, no, Elijah was not being a selfish jester. Instead, through him, God was establishing a principle. We must take care of his work first, not after doing what we think we need to do.

Elijah said that he would prove that his request was from God. "Thus saith the Lord God of Israel the barrel of meal shall not waste neither shall the cruise of oil fail until the day that the Lord sendeth rain upon the earth I Kings 17:14."

The widow did just as Elijah had told her. She trusted the Word of God through the man of God. And what Elijah had promised her did, indeed, come to pass. The Bible says, "The barrel of meal wasted not, neither did the cruise of oil fail, according to the word of the Lord which he spake by ElijahI Kings 17:16."

Here is the kicker for us. Jesus said, "There were many Widows in Israel at that time of Elias when the heavens were shut up three years six months when great famine was throughout all the land. But unto none of them was Elias sent *except to this one*" (Luke 4:25–26, emphasis added). Only *one* was visited and taken care of.

If you, too, dare to step out and obey the Word without any reservations, then you will be the only one favored, even though many times it may not appear to be fair to others. Amen.

We return now to the weather report for Community Day, under the umbrella of "from prediction to prayer." After all the weather predictions had been made, I prayed this to God:

> God, this is not for our enjoyment, but for the community, that we may reach out to the people thereof. This endeavor is at Your command, to go ye highways and hedges. compel them to come in, that our house may be full.

Pray the Word

Sometimes we become keenly aware that the Enemy is moving into a situation, trying to thwart the plans and purposes of God. But this is a time to be reminded that Jesus gave us authority. "All power is given unto me … Go ye" (Matthew 28:19).

In the week prior to Community Day, one of our churchwomen was praying for our nation's president: "Lord, he has the authority, but let him take the authority and use it for good." Those words stuck in my spirit, and the Lord said to me, "You have the authority. I have given it to you. Just use the authority I have given you. Here is the example."

And He gave me the example of Jesus in a boat with His disciples. There came a storm that was raging as the rains poured and the winds blew against the boat. There was no question that He, the Son of God, had authority over everything. He stood up and exercised the authority He had over the wind and the rains, speaking, "Peace be still Mark 4:39," and the storm ceased.

Jesus, when He was getting ready to leave earth and ascend to heaven, said, essentially, "All power is given to me, and so now I send you." Recognize that Jesus calls us to go to the people of all nations and teach them to know Him and live for Him. He gives us everything we need to do what He has called us to do.

In addition, anything that goes against what He has commanded us to do is satanic, and He has given us the authority to take control in those situations. So let us claim our authority and take control.

From Prediction to Prayer

I know that I wasn't the only one praying that the weather come under subjection for Community Day. Oh the power of agreement! Jesus said that if any two or three are gathered in His name, then not only would He be there, but He would also be touching our hearts and agreeing with us. He will give us what we ask.

As I was in and out of the rain all week long, I prayed, "Lord, don't let it rain on Community Day." It would cloud up and rain again and again. At one point, I stood on my deck, looking out over it and into the sky, commanding the clouds to go away. It was the inverse of what Elijah did when his people needed rain. The same principle applies.

Faith Lesson with Elijah

We must be in tune with God's timing of his plans and purposes. Ecclesiastes 3 reminds us, "To everything there is a season, a time to every purpose under the heaven." After this Scripture lists all of the things that time brings about, verse 11 says, "And He has made everything beautiful in His time."

First Kings 18:42–45 records the time when Elijah prayed and sent his servant to look for signs of rain. When the servant returned, he had nothing new to report. He had seen nothing indicative of rain. Let's not forget that it had not rained in many years—not a sprinkle, not a drop, not even a cloud. But we also have to remember, "Faith is evidence of things not seen Hebrews 11:1 ." Elijah told the servant to go again. Again nothing to report. Faith is also "substance of things hoped for Hebrews 11:1," so Elijah told his servant to go and look again.

How weary the servant must have been climbing that hill over and over, only to come back with another bad report. He was probably asking himself, *What's the use? It has not rained in over three years. Why should we think that things are going to change?* Can you feel his weariness? Can you identify? God has made promises, but the servant is not seeing any results. With God's promises, we sometimes make predictions that are contrary to those promises. In fact, our predictions sometimes delay the promises' manifestation. But we trudge the road anyway, weary, hoping for a change, realizing that it could happen, but in actuality not seeing any point in returning again to look.

But Elijah tells his servant to go back and look seven times. On his seventh trip, the servant returns with a skip in his step—not because he had seen rain, but because he had seen evidence of it—"a cloud the size of a man's handI Kings 18: 44."

Elijah sent word to the king before the rain came. He acted out of faith, with evidence of things not seen. "And it came to pass in the meanwhile that the heavens were black with clouds and winds and ... there was a great rain I Kings 18:45." Faith's substance and evidence became manifest.

My Church's Community Day

On Friday evening the rain stopped, even though the prediction for Saturday was an afternoon thunderstorm. When I and some others came out early that morning, we saw men working diligently to set up the things we needed for Community Day.

Faith without works is dead. These men didn't stand around waiting to see if there was any possibility of rain; instead, they put their faith into action and behaved as if it were not going to rain.

Faith lesson: Walk by faith, not by sight.

What a wonderful day Community Day turned out to be. It was just beautiful. The ministries were at their best. Many came to this event, as many had registered to take part.

God's weather report is not the same as humankind's, because He controls the weather.

From Prediction to Prayer, Revisited

There are times when God chooses to thwart the predictions of what could have and should have been. He does this in response to people's prayers.

Faith lesson: Hold on to the horns of the altar by holding on to the Word and promises of God. No matter *what* (the immediate conditions) you see or *how* you see it (your opinion of it), faith is still the substance of things hoped for. No rain on Community Day was evidence of things not seen. The sun will shine!

Sometimes we are so quick to say of Elijah, "He had a lot of faith. I don't have that much yet. I'm not there yet." Let's look at what the Bible has to say on this matter. "Elijah was a man subject to passions as we are James 5:17". . He was no different than we; he just chose to obey and believe God and to use the authority that God had given him.

Prayer Is the Lifeline in Your Holding Pattern

Just as the aeronautical holding pattern is an actual course charted by the pilot, your complete journey is orchestrated by God. If you have gone off your charted course, then the possibilities of completing your journey are almost nil. So let's take time to look at whether or not you have what you need to finish the journey.

CHAPTER 7

Completing Your Journey

· · · · · · · · · · · · · · · ·

*"Looking unto Jesus, the author and **finisher**..."Hebrews 12:2*

It is so easy to get waylaid along our journey. We desire to stop, so we often settle for less than we could have received. It's very important to make sure that we do not lose heart again. This chapter includes some foundational things we need to know.

Everyone Has a Purpose and a Destiny

Having purpose means resolutely aiming at a specific goal and working toward a specific end that is worked out over the course of seasons (Ecclesiastes 3:1).

Having destiny means that God has purposed you to go in a particular direction toward the completion of your journey. It is He who determines events and brings about the fulfillment of your purpose.

We are a destined people. Jesus said, "I've come that you might have life and that [life] more abundantly John 10:10." We are not destined merely to exist day-by-day, nor are we made to stumble around, hoping that we eventually hit the mark and accomplish God's purpose for us.

Once in a while, it's good that we stop and evaluate the journey that the Lord has placed us on.

Let's use two geographical places in the Bible as examples to learn a spiritual lesson.

> And Terah took Abram his son, and Lot the son of Haran his son's son, and Sarai his daughter in law, his son Abram's wife; and they went forth with them from Ur of the Chaldees, to go into the land of Canaan … and they came to Haran and dwelt there … and the days of Terah were two hundred and five years; and *Terah died in Haran* (Genesis 11:31–32, emphasis added).

Terah (Abram's father) lived in a country called Ur of which he left to go to Canaan a land which we know later as the Promised Land, but for reasons the Bible does not say, he stopped instead at the village of Haran. The Bible says that he *settled* in this land , lived for 205 years, and died. We can, like Terah who physically stopped in a land and settle there instead of going on to the land of Cannaan of which we know as the Promised land. He settle for less and miss God's best.

How often we start our journey knowing where we are going and confident of what God has purposed for our lives, but along the way we slow down because things intervene in our lives. It is then we start settling for less.

There is a difference between going through a season and staying in a season. We go through a season in our journey and continue on until we are through. If we stop somewhere else and refuse to continue, however, we will be found settling for less. For instance, there is the *season* of raising children, which might seem to slow you down. Your priorities must change. Sometimes there is a season where your job changes or you lose your job. However, you are not to become stuck in that season where the status of your purpose changes from delayed to unfruitful. Here, again, you must know the difference between getting stuck and abiding in God's holding pattern. It is also important to note that your predetermined destination may be canceled if you are not careful. A little farther down, read the account of Lot, whose destination was canceled because he went off in another direction.

Even in the difficult season you are going through, you are working out your purpose and can be fruitful. I was called to teach when my children were born. My gift led me in teaching the children, and thus my purpose continued. I didn't settle, as Terah did, into a "spirit of retirement" after my children grew up; instead, I moved into *my next level in ministry*.

The Key Here Is Balance
Having balance in your life means never forgetting what God has purposed you to do as you go through each season of your life. Understand that your purpose is worked out in seasons. Just as winter follows fall, spring follows winter, and summer follows spring, each season of your life flows into and becomes the next.

There is fall, when the trees lose most of which makes them beautiful. Then there is winter, where everything appears dead. Some seasons are enjoyable and others are nearly unbearable, but we must go through each one in order to get to the season of harvest. Your purpose is worked out in seasons, and just as the earth needs each season to accomplish the purpose of producing crops for harvest, your life relies on its seasons to accomplish God's purpose for you. If you do not keep your focus on God during each season, then it will become easy for you to forget all about the purpose/ministry to which God has called you—and thereby to forget your destiny, as well.

Terah settled in Haran, and "there he died."

Settling for less means that your dreams die.

Seasons are so important to God's purposes. Therefore, the question becomes this: How do I keep from becoming stuck in a dormant season so I won't end up settling for less?

First, I give you a warning: it is dangerous to leave your dormant season before its fulfillment. Even if springtime is here and the apples are on the tree, you must not pick them before they are ripe, or else they are no good to you or anyone else.

The Bible confirms this in Philippians 4:6 "Be anxious for nothing ... everything by prayer and supplication make your requests known unto God."

Next, know that God orchestrates the seasons. In a season of apparent latency, you will see that God is still using you, but at a different level or in a different way, the specifics of which you may not yet understand. God will *stir up* your gift in this season. And the Lord expects you, of course, to use it. The Bible says, your gift makes room for you, and we are to be instant in season (when the time is apparent) and out of season" 2 Timothy 4:2when it appears that it is not the time. You are expected to be obedient. However, when you are *not using* your gift, you are being disobedient. If you are disobedient, then you will begin to notice that you feel uncomfortable, restless, and dissatisfied. You will feel like Jeremiah the prophet; after he felt discouraged, he decided that he would never speak again. He said that the *Word in him* became "fire shut up in his bones Jeremiah 20:9."

If you consistently ignore your gift, failing to use or walk in it, then you are disobedient. Then a progression begins. Disobedience can move you into doubt of God and into disbelief of your purpose in Him.

Your disobedience, however, will not stop the plans of God. He can and will raise up someone else to complete what He had given you to do.

While still at Haran, after Terah had settled for less, the Lord spoke to *Abram* instead, whom He chose to achieve His eternal purposes. If you don't obey God, then He will raise up someone who will. In the Bible, God raised up a generation that would obey him."

Remember that the children of Israel wandered in the wilderness for forty years because of their disobedience and unbelief. They wandered until the entire first generation died and a brand new generation was "raised up." It was this following generation that entered into the Promised Land.

On your journey, it is crucial to know that you will have choices. Let's go back to the story of Abram, which now includes Lot.

> And there was a strife between the herdsmen of Abram's cattle and the herdsmen of Lot's cattle. And Abram said to Lot, let there be no strife, I pray thee, between me and thee and between my herdsmen and thy herdsmen; for we be brethren. Is not the whole land before thee ... And Lot lifted up his eyes and beheld all the plain of Jordan, and it was well watered everywhere, before the Lord destroyed Sodom and Gomorrah. Then Lot chose him all the plain of Jordan. (Genesis 13:7–11)

Lot had a choice to make. Although previously walking in purpose and in the right direction, he came to a crossroads and chose to walk away from the path of purpose. What caused him to make this choice? He was governed by "the lusts of the eyes." The Bible says that Lot took a long look at the "fertile plains of the Jordan Valley in the direction of Zoar" (Genesis 13:10). He beheld that the whole area was well watered, everywhere he looked. It was *like* the garden of the Lord and the beautiful land of Egypt. *Oh Egypt.*

Be careful of the word *like,* as it indicates a familiar spirit. Like the Spirit of God, the familiar spirit will prompt you to do things. The difference between the two is that the familiar spirit appeals more to the flesh. *What you see isn't always what you will get.*

Also note that Lot chose this land for *himself.* That was his next great temptation, to operate in pride (best expressed in, "What's in it for me and mine?"), as Lot didn't care what others were left with.

What you see is not always what you get.

Abram, by way of contrast, did not always know where he was going, but he was led by the Spirit of God and was motivated by love. Love "seeketh not her own" (1 Corinthians 13:5), which means that love seeks what is best for others in God.

Abram essentially said to Lot, "Take your choice of any section of land. Have what you want." There is a lesson here. Abram displayed wisdom in this situation. Even though he had brought Lot with him on his journey, he released him when he left Haran.

There is another lesson to be learned here: *Be careful whom you surround yourself with.* When you help others, make sure your actions align with your purpose and destiny. When God separates people from your life, let them go. *Don't ever be a follower of someone else's choice when it does not connect with the purpose that the Lord has given you and with your destiny.* Jesus said, "Pick up your cross daily and follow meMatthew 16:24." Follow Him, not others.

The Blessings of Obedience

In Genesis 13:12, we learn that Abram stayed in the land of Canaan (the Promised Land). Lot moved his tents to a place near Sodom. After Lot was gone, God promised Abram a destiny.

"And the Lord said to Abram, after that Lot was separated from him Lift up your eyes and look from the place where thou art northward and southward and eastward and westward: For all the land which thou seest, to thee will I give it and to thy seed forever" (Genesis 13:14–15).

God told Abram to get up and walk throughout the whole land, its length and breadth. Abram obeyed. He removed his tent and dwelt in the plain of Mamre, where he built an altar to the Lord.

I imagine that Abram, at this point, felt wonderfully about his accomplishments. He had obeyed God. Thereby, we learn that making right choices honors the God who calls us out to make a great journey. Abram recognized Him by building an altar to Him.

Abram may have been thinking, *Finished with this phase of my life, I am waiting to hear further instructions on how to go forward.*

Have you ever thought that a particular phase of your life was over? You feel that you're going forward, but then something happens. You find yourself having to stop right where you are. You feel that the pause button has once again been pressed and that you have to step backward in order to resolve an issue you thought should have been done with already.

Though separating Abram and Lot was necessary, God was not yet through with Lot. He wanted to use Abram to extend His grace and mercy to him.

At this time, the Bible records that there was a war between the countries. Lot was caught up in it. He was captured and lost all that he had.

On your journey, you may have to go a little deeper into your human relationships. Being separated from someone does not mean that your love for him or her is extinguished. Abram, after Lot lost everything, demonstrated *love* toward—and, indeed, personified love for—Lot.

Genesis 14 tells us that after Lot was captured and lost all he had, Abram went and fought for him, restoring all that had been lost.

Love: Abram could have continued on his way, saying to himself, *I told Lot. He made the choice; now let him suffer the consequences.* But instead, he chose to fight for his loved one.

On this journey, you will have to fight and engage in spiritual warfare. Abram fought for someone else's victory as much as he fought to defeat Lot's enemy. "Greater love have no man than this … than a man lay down his life for a friend John 15:13."

Let us meditate upon what Jesus did for us. While we were yet in our sins, Christ died for us. "The wages of sin is death but the gift of God is eternal life Romans 6:23

." Out of the love the Father has for us, He sacrificed His only Son so that we may have eternal life. Our God is "He who spared not his own son Romans 8:32." Also, "God so loved the world that he gave his only begotten son, that whosoever believeth in him shall not perish, but have everlasting life" (John 3:16).

Love Manifested

A pastor friend of mine fasted three days and three nights in order to help a fellow man. His was a soul that the Enemy was trying to destroy by keeping him back from accepting the Lord. "Greater love have no man than this," however. This pastor afflicted his soul with fasting and prayer to win the battle for the other man's soul. The great weapons of fasting and prayer will defeat the Enemy every time.

Paul reminded the people of the church at Corinth, "The weapons of our warfare are not carnal but mighty through God pulling down the strongholds and everything that exalted itself ....2 Cor. 10:4."

We will experience warfare when the Enemy comes to discourage us and tries to make us stop. Aren't you glad that God gives us weapons to fight with, so that we can complete our journey even in the midst of this warfare?

Know who your Enemy is. Know the Enemy of your purpose and destiny, the one who is trying to keep you from completing your journey. There will be many times when you experience what appears to be a setback but look at those times not as roadblocks but as "sidebars" to your ministry—things which, along your way, God leads you to accomplish. It will be with joy when you stop, take the time to help someone else, and perhaps place that person back on his or her own journey.

Remember what the song says: "Love lifted me." You are expected to lift someone else in love. This is not an interruption of your journey. This is not a withholding of time and a delay of your purpose. In fact, it is opposite those things. When you are in a holding pattern, you are still in a position to minister.

When in my own holding pattern, God gave me a vision.

I saw a concrete slab and a *V* shape. I but briefly saw the sections of concrete, but at the end of them was the *V,* and within the lines forming the *V* was a small plant growing. Surrounding it were dead stalks, but within the dead stalks, it was green. In spite of the hardness of the concrete and the deadness of the surrounding stalks, the small plant grew.

The Lord spoke to me and said, "Where *you* are, there is life. In spite of where you are, you are growing, even though it is a place not at all conducive to growth. Everything that touched the concrete, including the stalks surrounding it, died, yet you are living. The dead stalks are your protection so that you don't touch that concrete. The stalks may be dead, but even this death protects you so that you can grow. You don't like the position you are in, but I have placed you there, and in spite of it, you are growing, surviving. You don't like that those around you are dead, but I'm using them, actually, to protect you. They are dead; don't expect life to come from them. But I'm using them for your good."

Dear Reader,

You may be the only one who is speaking life. Though surrounded by death and disappointments, and virtually nothing else, you can still grow. In spite of your environment and circumstances, the hardness of them, He has allowed you to be here.

The Lord will even use your negative surroundings to be of help to you, to protect you so that you can become what He has called you to be. You will get to where He has ordained you to be.

Sitting on the plane of despair, let your light shine, even though you are surrounded by impatience, despair, and hopelessness. God has placed you here on purpose. He paused your journey so that you may do many things necessary in your life of which you are not aware, and also so that you may be of help to someone else.

But allow nothing to stop you from completing your journey.

CHAPTER 8

Sickness—A Seat in *The Pattern* None of Us Likes to Sit

• • • • • • • • • • • • • • • •

Has God got you "on hold" while you endure sickness? When you experienced the first attack of illness, *you prayed.* You went to the altar *for prayer.* You followed the dictates of the old saying: You prayed and *it* stayed; you fasted and *it* lasted.

You know that God is a healer. He has healed you in the past, and you have seen Him answer others' prayers for healing, too.

Say your illness returns or else just remains with you, like an unmovable rock or a tree that has dug its roots deep into the ground and" shall not be moved" You feel like you are buckled into a seat on a plane or in an isolated cabin because you cannot do things like you used to. Your sickness has become a hindrance to your functioning and mobility, as well as to your journey. You feel that no one understands your pain.

People now just smile slightly when they pass you by, and they pass you by because they are at a loss for words. The Word has been spoken to and over you so many times, and yet you remain sick. You think, *God, are you really hearing me?*

I actually added this chapter after I had completed this book. All my life, I had been in very good health. My trials, like anyone else's, were varied, but sickness was never one of them. I was the one known to take care of others when they were sick, even when I was a child and sickness came into my family's home. I was the one who took care of my mother and sisters as they went through various illnesses and surgeries.

Then I had an attack of excruciating pain. Arthritis of the knee was my diagnosis—extreme arthritis in my left knee, to be exact. One day I found I could not walk; I could not put any weight on that knee. Inflammation was causing my pain, the doctor had said.

Applying ice packs, taking anti-inflammatory drugs, and drinking natural juice was supposed to eliminate the inflammation. Home remedies and painful exercises were part of my daily regimen. It was a necessary pattern I had to repeat in order to get my body back into the condition I had enjoyed before.

My knee became the best weather forecaster. When I thought I had been delivered and that things had returned to normal, a change in the weather informed me, "Not so." I, who once ran through airports and walked up hills and down hills in Africa to minister, was now immobilized. No longer did I run upstairs and walk two to three miles a day. Now I hopped.

I would pray and thank God for relief, but then my knee's condition would degrade as soon as the weather changed. "O God," I cried, "how can I continue my journey in the ministry when I can't even walk around the block?"

The things I loved most were now unreachable. For instance, I had always attended the 5:00 a.m. prayer service at my church, but now I could not climb up the stairs and reach the upper room where it was held without experiencing pain.

I was becoming a hostage to pain. Immobility was fast becoming a part of my life, but I did not welcome it *at all*. One day I simply broke down and cried out to God, "Am I finished, at this time and at my age, with the work that I so love?"

Having limited mobility is like having a reserved seat on a plane. Though it is possible for you to move from cabin to cabin and from seat to seat, there are boundaries that you are unable to cross. You are bound to remain in a certain area. Your ticket restricts you to only one seat in one section of the aircraft. Given my limited mobility, when I attempt to move from one place to another, the pain flares up. It is like having a flight attendant reminding me that I cannot go any further. I must stay in my assigned place.

All possibilities of moving forward, even in this restricted environment, seem to be null. Do I just settle into my seat and never move from the place where I am allowed to be? It is so easy to do just that. However, as you know, arthritis is not something that just goes away by one's sitting and waiting. *Immobility works against arthritis*. Though I am *limited* in what I do, because of pain, I *have to* move within my ability to do so, many times pressing past the pain to move even more. My range of motion is limited, but I must work within that range, ever expecting more movement—or so my physical therapist told me.

At times like these, what I always say is,…. "Speak, Lord."

Ah, once again I think of the holding pattern and its definition. Though it is a *state of waiting,* it is a flying *pattern* oval in shape, wherein the craft makes a series of 360-degree turns. My physical therapist told me what I had to do to improve my mobility: I had to move toward achieving things of which I was capable. After a few visits to the physical therapist, I noted improvement, slow but progressive. When I arrived for one of my appointments, I was told that it would be my last.

Oh my, how disappointed I was. I thought that my therapy would be ongoing until the knee pain left and I was as mobile as before. Immediately I had this sinking feeling. "There is no more hope. They can't do any more for me. That's why they have stopped my visits."

My physical therapist somewhat alleviated my fears when she said that this was my last *supervised* visit. She said that I had to continue doing what she had taught me to do. In order for me to become mobile again, I had to take responsibility and *continue making the pattern*—the oval shape (moving my knee around in a circle). Continue the exercise, she told me, and use the ice compress. Moving onto the next stage, I should use weights to make my knee and leg more pain-resistant (which, ironically, meant that I had to endure more pain). I also needed to lose weight, she told me.

For every pound of fat a person loses, four pounds of pressure are taken off the knees, my physical therapist said. Now, I had been in a yo-yo pattern for years: losing weight, gaining weight, losing weight, gaining weight.

Okay, Lord, I hear you. "Lay aside *every weight* and the sin that so easily besets us and run the race with *patience.* Looking to Jesus the author and finisher of our Faith" Heb 12:1 (emphasis added). Our purpose is stated in Hebrews 12:2, and now I saw that any improved mobility would depend on my following this pattern. The pattern now takes on purpose: "And I can do all things through Christ who gives me the strength" (Philippians 4:13).

My recovery was now up to me. Stop right there. It is up to me? Talk about feeling like cold water had been dumped on the fire of anticipation. Even though the promise of the above Scripture rang resoundingly in my spirit, I sure wasn't edified by it, given my track record of inconsistency in the area of my own health. However, the promise that my physical therapist gave me, that she would be available for consultation when needed, shone a fresh light. Is that not like the Lord? He lays the foundation and opens up the way, but we have to make the decision to "walk therein"—or, as a popular sport shoe company expresses it, I have to "just do it."

Hebrews 12:1 says, "Seeing we are compassed about with so great a cloud of witnesses." I allow my Holy Ghost imagination to take over. I imagine hearing the voices of those who have gone on before us (the cloud of witnesses) cheering me on. "You can make it, you can do this, we did it ... and He was always there for us." It's up to me! I can't quit continuing along in the pattern that He has allowed to develop in my life *for my good*. "Rejoice in Hope; be patient in afflictions; be persistent in prayer" (Romans 12:12 CSB).

CHAPTER 9

Promises *In* Perseverance

. . . .

'"Keeping the Word of His Patience" Revelations 3:10

At the end of last year, one day I was reading , Revelation 3:3–17. During my quiet time with the Lord, God gave me a word to ponder. The word was *perseverance*.

> And to the angel of the church in Philadelphia write: These thing saith he that is holy, he that is true, he that has the key of David, he that openeth and no man shutteth: and shutteth and no man open.

> I know thy works: behold, I have set before you an open door and no man can shut: for thou has a little strength and has kept my word and has not denied my name.

> Behold I will make them of the synagogue of Satan, which say they are Jews, and are not, but do lie; behold I will make them to come and

worship before thy feet and know that I have loved thee.

Because thou has kept the word of my patience, I will also keep thee from the hour of temptation which shall come upon the whole world to try them that dwell upon the earth.

Behold I come quickly hold that fast which thou hast that no man take thy crown

Him that overcometh will I make a pillar in the temple of my God; and he shall go no more out; and I will write upon him the name of my God,

He that hath an ear, let him hear what the Spirit saith unto the churches. (Revelation 3:7–13)

In the tenth verse, Jesus says, "You kept the word of my patience," which means, "You kept my command to persevere."

Do you know that *God commanded us to persevere?* In the above passage of Scripture, He shares with us some of the promises of perseverance.

The Promises of Perseverance

To be exact, it was the last Sunday of the year when the Lord spoke this word to me. The end of the year is always a time for reflection, when we look back and review how we handled things in the past year. We are proud of many of our decisions, and we wish that we would have handled some things differently. Hindsight is always greater than present sight. But the present is just that, and we do the best we can with what we have in making any decision presently.

Sometimes we make decisions prayerfully, sometimes spontaneously, sometimes according to our past experiences that didn't work out for the best, and sometimes by consulting or just talking to someone else. How we regret a lot of our decisions. Like using some of those home remedies, sometimes what we did was a real waste of time.

Receiving council, or advice from others which sometimes just tells you to stop going in the direction you are going. Change directions might work out better. You quit going in the direction that you believe is right because of their advice. If it is not the plans of the Lord for you, receiving advice from others, can be like following the scapegoat into the slaughterhouses of yesteryear. My mother told me the method whereby sheep would be sent to slaughter in Chicago in days of old. A lead goat would lead the sheep up to a certain spot. When the goat arrived at that place, it would jump to the side and up onto a shelf—as the goat had been trained to do—while the sheep would all fall into the slaughterhouse to be killed.

The arms of flesh will fail you. Have you ever had another person agree with you, leading you to believe that the two of you were going all the way together, only for that person to jump to the side and leave you out there all by yourself?. It is so easy to start depending and leaning on others . When that person fails to be what you expected or what they promised you and if you had your focus on that person instead of the Lord, you will oftimes just feel like quitting after that betrayal.

This is just a part of life and will be real experiences but never reasons to justify quitting

However, at any time during our difficulties, bad experiences, poor decisions, and dealing with what life has handed us, we still have the option of quitting. Quitting is just like sitting in our seats on the airplane, remaining in the same place and doing nothing. many have.

Therefore, quitting takes different forms. *Outright* quitting consists of not taking another step; doing nothing else; stopping; and coming to a place of resignation. In this case, we go off in another direction, one different from the direction chosen for us by God.

Occupying space is another form of quitting. In doing this, one behaves as the stubborn child who stamps his or her foot and says, "I am not moving from this spot—and you can't make me."

How do we know when a person has quit? Well, in his or her life there is no evidence of positive results and personal growth, because the person has given no effort.

Again, a wise person looks back in reflection and becomes honest about having quit.

Do you persevere regardless of the pain, circumstance, etc., in which you find yourself?

In the passage of Scripture above, the Lord commands us to *persevere*. What does *persevere* mean? We already know its opposite: to quit. So, let's take a look at what it is, now that we have learned what it is not.

One biblical definition of *persevere* is "to stand after you have done all." *Stand,* Ephesians says.

- ▲ Determine not to go backward, but instead press on toward the mark of the high calling, which is God's call on your life. Waver not, no matter the circumstances.
- ▲ Pursue what is right and do all you can no matter how bad things look. No amount of negative influence must stop your pursuit to do things God's way.
- ▲ Set goals, fulfilling each objective with those goals in view. Resolve to follow through, no matter how long it may take.

The lyrics to the hymn "Higher Ground" say,

> I'm pressing on the upward way,
> New heights I'm gaining every day;
> Still praying as I onward bound,
> *Lord, plant my feet on higher ground.*

The higher ground is not ever a position or title we should try to attain. Instead, it's the highest place in Him. It's "the mark" of "press toward the mark of the high calling in Christ Jesus. Philippians 3:14"

In Revelation 3, John speaks to the church at Philadelphia, the church of love, which is reflective of the church age we are in now, reportedly. Many Christians believe, in light of the time line of the book of Revelation that the rapture is described in chapters three and four.

Historically, Philadelphia was a small-town faithful church established to be a center of Greek culture. The town was renowned for its surrounding vineyards, but it was subject to frequent earthquakes. I find this interesting, because one of the signs that the last days have arrived is earthquakes in diverse places. But at this geographical location, earthquakes were the norm, so the congregants wouldn't have been too shaken when they experienced a tremor.

This in and of itself can be a dangerous thing. If something becomes too familiar to you, then you are not as cautious in the face of it. Neither are you as likely to prepare yourself for what could be a disastrous event, *especially in these last days.*

Peter's second epistle warned of the mockery Christians will experience in the last days. He said, "There will be scoffers walking after their own lusts" (2 Peter 3:3), people concerned only with themselves. These people will not seek to please anyone else; they will act in their own selfish interests.

This is what the scoffers will say to the faithful: "Where is the promise of his coming? For since the fathers fell asleep, all things continue as they were from the beginning of the creation" (2 Peter 3:4). But those people who had long ago said that were deceived. They had forgotten, as Peter went on to say, about the flood and about how Noah warned people for 120 years that it was coming. The people consistently ignored him, and as a result they were all consumed in one great swoop.

Back to the church at Philadelphia: Jesus commends them for their faithfulness. The most important thing that counts to God is your being faithful. He is not impressed with numbers like we are, nor is He impressed with time, the past events of our lives. What we should want to hear Him say is, "Well done, [my] good and faithful servant Matthew 25:21."

In the past, were you faithful to the call that God placed on your life? If you are going to enjoy the promises of *perseverance,* then you must be *faithful.*

To this church—as to the rest of the churches addressed in Revelation 2 and 3—Jesus says, "I know thy works. Revelation 2:2" He does *not* say, "I know thy attendance." Even though some Christians have a record of good attendance at church, their works do not reflect their faith. Some people know that it's right to come to church, but their failure to perform works and to work out their soul's "salvation with fear and trembling,Phlippians 2:14" "knowing that the time is short, I Corinthians 7:29" and "redeeming the time, Ephesians 5:16" as Paul told the people at three different churches, displeases God greatly.

Jesus admires the church at Philadelphia not because the people are hallmarks of strength and are great in their accomplishments, but because they have had "little strength Revelations 3:8" but still kept His Word.

You have probably experienced times when you didn't think you were going to make it through an illness or a different problem that had almost consumed you, but somehow you *pressed on* despite the difficulty, and in so doing you learned that *in your weakness, His strength was made perfect*—and therefore you learned to depend on His strength, not your own.

When I read Revelation 3:8, I said, "God, thank you for the little strength you've given me, which was just enough to carry me through. Oh, but I found out it wasn't me who was strong; it was you."

When you supply whatever you have, God takes up the slack and supplies whatever else you need. You find that you are able to do some things that, if not for the Lord's helping you, you otherwise would not have been able to do. Though the steps you take might be painful, He is there to help you take each and every step—not all at once, but step-by-step, miraculously through His power.

I have found Him to be more than enough.

The key to pleasing God in your infirmity or trial is, given your little strength, not giving place to the Enemy. And if you fall because you aren't strong, then you get up and persevere thereafter. God is pleased with you during these times because, as Jesus says in the Scripture, "You kept my word and did not deny my name Revelation 3:8."

The church always has the greatest opportunity to keep His Word and refrain from compromising in light of economic situations or party affiliations. It teaches us how we will benefit if we keep Jesus as Lord of all our decisions. "Acknowledge Him in all your ways Proverbs 3:6." The church teaches us not to deny His name, as in refusing to do so results in God's being pleased with us.

Now I will elucidate the promises of perseverance. There are three in the above passage of Scripture.

First Promise of Perseverance

The first promise you will receive if you persevere is opportunity. Jesus says, "I have set before thee an open door that no man can shut Revelation 3:7." In the coming years, God is going to open doors that no person can shut.

Second Promise of Perseverance, from Revelation 3:9

The second promise, if you persevere, is that your enemies will be defeated. God will make "of the synagogue of Satan" those who say they are of Him but who are not. Instead, they are liars—your enemies. He will make those people come and worship at your feet, and they are going to know that *He loves you.* In other words, you should not worry about those who are trying to restrict you and hold you back, seemingly preventing you from achieving your goals. He is going to deal with them. Not to worry: He is going to make your enemies your footstool. "If a man's ways please the Lord. He will make his enemies be at peace with him. Proverbs 16:7."

Third Promise of Perseverance, from Revelation 3:10

The third promise is that Christ will preserve you until He comes again. "I will keep you in the hour of temptation," the Lord says. It is not merely tests and trials you go through—"*the light affliction that is for a moment*" (emphasis added)—but it is something indicative of what will come upon the whole earth during the great tribulation.

The climactic trials described in Matthew 24:6, 8, 10 and in the chapters of Revelation are delivered to you so that you may become perfect in Christ and in so doing count yourself worthy to escape. When we persevere in Christ, we escape damnation.

Clearly perceive the signs of the times. He says, "Behold I will come quickly. Him that overcometh.. Revelation 3: 11,12 Christ will give all the riches of heaven. He still orders your steps. No matter what you are going through, you can be an overcomer.

Arthritis is not an affliction for which you can take a pill for and be rid of. A part of my persevering with arthritis is doing physical therapy. The therapist moves me out of my comfort zone from a place where I nurse my feelings and *remain immobile,* because it will hurt if I move.

Mobility is my target. I'm limited in my mobility, but within those limitations, my physical therapist makes me move. This is not unlike having a reserved seat on a plane. I'm limited in where I can go, but I can move within the allotted space. If I am in a window seat, then it takes effort for me to squeeze past the person sitting next to me in order to get to the aisle. And if the airline attendants are serving, then I have to wait until they finish with an entire section before I can continue.

You cannot be an overcomer unless you *move* toward the goal of overcoming. It is not easy, because there are likely many obstacles in your way. These make you want to quit and ask, "What's the use?"

Physical therapy hurts. I have to stretch those muscles that tend to atrophy for lack of use, but I persevere because I know that, even though it is painful, ultimately it is the best thing for me. And if I persevere, then I notice that I become more mobile. Those things that were almost impossible before, I now take in stride.

Within the holding pattern, there is room to do that which is necessary while I'm waiting for God to heal me, deliver me, and set me free from these physical restraints. I mustn't quit, regardless of what my physical body is saying to me. I tell my body to line up with the Word of God. Healing is part of the children of God's bread. This holding pattern of illness will not prevent me from doing the will of God in my life or from reaching my destination.

I don't know about you, but this is a wonderful Word to me. Some things I have been through this past year made me want to quit, but the Lord spoke to me several times and confirmed that I was not to give up. He is so faithful.

Many people advised me to quit. It would have been far easier for me, that's for sure. Even the temptation just to maintain, to settle in right where I was and do nothing, was strong—but that is not perseverance.

God has commanded us to persevere. I didn't know that until I researched the Scripture after He spoke it to me that morning.

I just want to obey Him and keep His Word regardless of outside circumstances. Now He has also promised distinct things for one's perseverance. I can go forward even in my restricted, limited abilities. God's purpose for my life is greater than this light affliction, and it will have more weight in glory. For this, too, will pass."

Chapter 10

Remembering Foundational Truths -- Promises Made to Us

. . . .

"And I say to you ... Peter, upon this rock I will build my church and the gates of hell shall not prevail against you. And I will give you the keys [authority] of the kingdom of heaven and whatsoever you bind on earth shall be bound in heaven and whatsoever you loose on earth shall be loosed in heaven" (Matthew 16:18–19).

This was Jesus' response to Peter's answer to the question expressed in Matthew 16:15: "Who do you say that I am?" Peter's response and great revelation was, "Thou are the Christ, the Son of the Living God" (Matthew 16:16).

The rock upon which Jesus said He would build His church was, of course, Himself, the Son of the living God. He would not build his church on Peter, for heaven's sake. We would have been in trouble if He had built His church on Peter, given what happened in Peter's life from that point forward. "For other foundation can no man lay than that is laid, which is Jesus Christ I Corinthians 3:11."

The truth recorded is, "The gates of hell shall not prevail against" His church. The gates of hell will come, but they can neither prevail nor last.

You are the church. Nothing that will come upon you that the Lord is not first aware of and has allowed. The great truth is that death—the gates of hell—cannot and will not last.

John wrote "The Revelation of Jesus Christ" on the Isle of Patmos. He is found weeping in Revelation 5:4 because "no man was found worthy to open the book [of life] or look inside." And one of the elders said to him, "Weep not: look, the Lion of the tribe of Judah, the Root of David, hath prevailed to open the book" (Revelation 5:5).

Jesus had paid the ultimate price. "Thou art worthy to take the book, and to open the seals thereof: for thou wast slain and has redeemed us to God by thy blood out of every kindred and tongue and people and nation. And has made us unto our God kings and priests and *we shall reign on the earth*" (Revelation 5:9–10, emphasis added).

We Are Overcomers

The promise is this: "To him that overcometh will I grant to sit with me in my throne, even as I also overcame, and am set down with my Father in his throne" (Revelation 3:21).

Here is our foundational truth: The gates of hell shall not prevail, because *He has prevailed.*

Know how and why your victory has been won. When you know that, you will not so easily give up, faint, or fall. *Prevail* means to gain the advantage; to be victorious; to triumph. This is your promise if you persevere.

Paul told the church at Rome, "We are more than conquerors through Him that love us Romans 8:37." Nothing, absolutely nothing, can separate us from His love. God so loves us that He gave us His very best: His only begotten Son.

What shall we, then, say to these things? Paul wrote, "If God be for us who can be against us? He that spared not his own Son but delivered him up for us all, how shall he not with him also freely give us all things" (Romans 8:31–32)?

Notwithstanding what we will go through, our trials and tribulations, we will prevail. "For his sake we are killed all the day long; accounted as sheep for the slaughter Romans 8:36." There is absolutely no need for a Christian to fear such an end, however, because "in all these things we are more than conquerors through him that loved us Romans 8:37."

Paul then provided the Romans—and us—with a list of extreme situations that would normally consume anyone. The question is, *What can separate us from His love?*

Neither death, nor life, nor angels, nor principalities, nor powers, nor things   present, nor things to come … Nor height nor depth, nor any creature shall be able to separate us from the love of God, which is in Christ Jesus our Lord Romans 8:38,39.

Because He prevailed, we can be overcomers.

Jesus built His church so that His people would be overcomers from the beginning. As we are the church, of the baptized body of believers, we are not built to fail. From the very beginning, you and I were made to be winners. Defeat is not written into your DNA if you are of the church.

In the beginning, Jesus spoke to Peter as an individual, *just as He is speaking to you.* He spoke the promise on His way to accomplish the victory. Now Revelation tells us of the promise's *fulfillment.*

Here it is, the wonderful, the tried and proven, news: we cannot be defeated because we are overcomers.

Look at what it says in Revelation 5:8: "When Jesus had taken the book ... the four beast and four and twenty elders fell down before the Lamb, having every one of them harps, and golden vials full of *odours,* which are the prayers of the saints and they sang a new song" (emphasis added). Prayer and praise are a sweet, fragrant incense to the Lord. "Let my prayer be set forth before you as incense and the lifting up of my hands as the evening sacrifice" (Psalm 141:2).

Prayer

Golden vials of odors are the prayers of the saints. This means that not one of my prayers is wasted—neither prayers that have been prayed on my behalf nor prayers that I myself have prayed. This is *a great place to take a praise break.*

I want to shout now. Not one prayer that *seems* to have fallen by the wayside, because the situation has gotten worse and it appears that God is silent, has been lost.

The harps represent praise. We should praise God not only after we have emerged from a difficult situation, but also during it, as prayer goes hand in hand with praise. Praise is comely to the people of God. Make sure you use this most powerful weapon along with your prayers. *The Lord inhabits the praises of Israel*, the Bible says; plus, we already know that "He promises never to leave us or forsake us … but praise manifest his presence … and in His presence is fullness of Joy evermore … The Joy of the Lord is the strength of his people" (Nehemiah 8:10).

In addition, our praise just might have to include a sacrifice—"lifting up my hand as the evening sacrifice Psalm 141:2"—but it's a sacrifice that is well pleasing to the Lord.

Remember who you are. He hath made us kings and priests to our God, to our overcomer, to the conqueror. We make up a royal priesthood adopted (specially chosen) into the royal family as the King's kids, proven by His love for us.

Jesus would not come down from the cross even though he suffered, bled, and died. The vail in the temple, once torn, gave us the privilege of having a personal relationship with God the Father. Christ's death provided us with direct access to the throne room of God, where we will find His grace to help us in our time of need.

Jesus spent three days in the tomb and descended into hell: He took *the keys,* the authority, back from Satan, thereby defeating the Enemy who will not, can no longer, prevail against us. After the victory was won, Christ left hell and the tomb. The psalmist David records the prophecy: "Lift up your head, O ye gates, and be ye lift up, ye everlasting doors; and the King of glory shall come in" (Psalm 24:7). David asks, "Who is this King of glory?" (Psalm 24:8). The answer is, "The Lord strong and mighty. The Lord mighty in battle" (Psalm 24:10). He is the conquering King, the King of glory. *We will prevail because He prevailed.*

Quitting is not even in my vocabulary. In no place within myself do I ever find that my answer is to quit.

As hard as it may seem to endure difficult trials, <u>no rock and no hard place takes me away from His purpose for me.</u> I remain in His hands while I am in His holding pattern. He has given me the grace needed to endure this season. And it all works together for my good.

When I reflect on my difficulties, I see that, yes, I have been between a rock and a hard place, but I have learned that <u>the rock is Jesus.</u> He is the solid rock onto which my anchor may hold. He is my foundation, the reason I can stand throughout the duration of a difficult experience. He is my confidence. He has my back; He doesn't allow me to fall back. The Holy Spirit becomes my teacher, and the God of miracles shows up.

There are certain laws in place that must be obeyed. The law of aerodynamics is one of them. If we obey it, then our aircraft will be able to remain in flight. But if we fail to obey that law, then we will fall to the earth. However, if we are to rise above that law and stay in the sky, then there must be a law that supersedes that of aerodynamics. That law is Christ.

The holding pattern is a charted pattern flown until there is a breakthrough enabling the plane to land. The holding pattern works, as it achieves its purpose.

But there is *someone* who supersedes the law of aerodynamics in your life's purpose and destiny. He knows how to hold *you*, not just your plans and purposes.

"Fear thou not; for I am with you: be not dismayed, for I am your God; I will strengthen you, yea, I will help you; yea, I will *uphold* you with the right hand of my righteousness" (Isaiah 41:10, emphasis added).

At last, we receive an announcement from the pilot: "The gate is open. The path is clear. We will be landing shortly."

At this point, sometimes the captain will tell you exactly what caused the delay, why it was necessary to fly in the holding pattern. Most times, however, the captain does not explain the reason, but only says, "It will be five minutes to the gate, and you will be able to depart the plane at that time."

The Red Sea just opened up; the miracle happened *suddenly*.

And if you remember Job, you recall that God never told him *why* he went through his terrible trials. The record reads that Job's "*latter end was greater than his beginning*" (Job 42:12, emphasis added), *which is extraordinary*. He received *double for his trouble*.

His blessings at the end of his life far exceeded his trials. His holding pattern, which allowed him to proceed to his destiny, was definitely worth his having taken the trip.

Job learned much about himself. He learned so much more about his God, as well. *How much have I learned about myself?* You never know what is in you until the test comes.

When God places you on hold, when you can no longer control the situation, let go and let God.

"Where can I go to flee from your presence ... If I take the wings of the morning behold thou art there ... Lord, thou hast been our dwelling place in all generations. Before the mountains were brought forth, or ever thou hadst formed the earth and the world, even from everlasting to everlasting, thou art God" (Psalm 90:1–2).

He has always been there, and He is God: sovereign, supreme, omnipotent, omnipresent. Yet within this great big God, I have found my own place through my relationship with Jesus Christ my Lord, in whom and where I can abide.

He that dwelleth in the secret place of the most High shall abide under the shadow of the almighty. I will say of the Lord, He is my refuge and my fortress: my God; in him will I trust. Surely he shall deliver thee from the snare of the fowler, and from the noisome pestilence. He shall cover thee with his feathers, and under his wings shalt thou trust; his truth shall be thy shield and buckler. (Psalm 91:1–4)

I can trust Him no matter *what* life dishes out to me and no matter *where* life takes me. I have the assurance that the "steps of a good man are ordered by the Lord ... and He delights in his way" (Psalm 37:23).

In *His* way, you might just find yourself in a holding pattern— taking a timeout, if you will, from the rigors of life, so that He can speak to you, teach you, refresh you, and lead you.

As I depart the plane with a little skip in my step—which might actually be a run to reach my connecting flight—I'm reminded to "run this race with patience Hebrews 12:1,"...... keeping my focus on Jesus, who is the author and *finisher* of my faith.

Wow, what a ride.

About the Author....

A Native of Chicago, Illinois, Dr. Herldleen Russell has traveled to Africa, Central and South America, Europe and throughout the United States as a speaker and teacher. She is an International Evangelist for the Church of God in Christ, Inc. Dr. Russell is a graduate of Moody Bible Institute in Chicago, Illinois and has a Doctorate of Divinity from Trinity Hall College and Seminary.

Once the Lord spoke to Dr. Russell and told her to "Ask for Africa," it was evident that the Lord's hand was enlarging her ministry. She has conducted Women's Conferences in Kenya and Uganda. Dr. Russell has hosted Conferences for Pastors throughout Uganda, Kenya and South Africa. The Dr. Herldleen Russell School of Ministry has graduated over 200 Pastors and has expanded to three campuses.

Dr. Russell and her teams have taken hundreds of pounds of clothing, shoes, and school supplies to the orphans of Uganda. They have also delivered over 1,000 pounds of medical supplies to clinics. The

Women's Conferences are also hosts of Women's Health Initiatives whereby medical personnel have joined her team. The initial building program built and furnished the first orphanage named for Dr. Ada Powell Marshall (former Supervisor of Greater MD First Jurisdiction COGIC). Bishop Lawrence Wooten extension for the school is finished along with other additions to the school in Mpigi, Uganda. A church in the village of Buyala is in its final stages of being completed along with a small school. Groundbreaking ceremony for the Dr. Willie Mae Rivers Educational Complex in Ibanda, Uganda has taken place to begin construction. The complex's projected completion date is in 2014. Sites for more schools and orphanages are also in the process of investigation to enhance the lives of the people of Uganda.

Dr. Herldleen Russell Ministries has partnered with the Water4 organization to bring clean water to Uganda's COGIC, villages, schools and orphanages. Water4 not only provides wells but training for the men of the villages to drill and maintain the wells, resulting in employment for the men.

Dr. Russell serves faithfully as the Supervisor of Women for the Church of God in Christ in both Uganda and Greater Maryland First Jurisdiction to implement the COGIC National Women's Department theme "Better Families...Better Schools...Better Communities...A Better World." She is humbled and excited about the opportunity to work with the Lord's people as a servant leader. Dr. Russell endeavors to train and encourage the women of God to take their rightful place in ministry utilizing their gifts to the glory of God.

Dr. Russell is married to Dr. Herbert J. Russell, Senior Pastor, Ridgley Ministries Church of God in Christ in Upper Marlboro, Maryland, *where she serves as Co-Pastor. She is the loving mother of five, the doting grandmother of 17 and one great grandchild, and praying Dr. Mom to thousands.*

….. TO GOD BE THE GLORY!

CPSIA information can be obtained at www.ICGtesting.com
Printed in the USA
BVOW05s0558050614

355407BV00001B/2/P